Restorative justice
The empowerment model

Restorative justice
The empowerment model

Charles K. B. Barton, PhD

HAWKINS PRESS
2003

Published in Sydney by:
    Hawkins Press
    A division of The Federation Press
    PO Box 45, Annandale, NSW, 2038
    71 John St, Leichhardt, NSW, 2040
    Ph (02) 9552 2200 Fax (02) 9552 1681
    E-mail: info@federationpress.com.au
    Website: http://www.federationpress.com.au

National Library of Australia
Cataloguing-in-Publication entry

    Barton, Charles K. B.
    Restorative justice: the empowerment model.

    Bibliography.
    Includes index.
    ISBN 1 87606 716 0

    1. Restorative justice. 2. Punishment – Philosophy
    I. Title.

364

Typeset by The Federation Press, Leichhardt, NSW.
    Printed by Southwood Press Pty Ltd, Marrickville, NSW.

Table of Contents

Preface

This book started out as a group conferencing manual, *Restorative Justice Conferencing: The Empowerment Model* (1997–1998) and it consolidates over ten years of work devoted to studying and teaching criminal justice. I began this work in 1990 as a PhD student at the Australian National University, arguing that substantial *victim empowerment* was urgently needed to put an end to the persistent and often horrendous revictimisation of the victim by the system.[1]

My encounter with restorative justice in 1995 was practical confirmation of victim empowerment in criminal justice. It also allowed me to see that offenders were no less disempowered by the system, and that their disempowerment was the greatest obstacle preventing them from putting things right with victims. This realisation prompted me to reconceptualise the entire criminal justice system in terms of *victim-offender empowerment* as its central principle. This book is yet the most developed articulation of what I call *the empowerment model of restorative justice*, and forms part of a wider *paradigm of empowerment* which encompasses both restorative and conventional criminal justice.[2]

My background for this work is both analytical and practical. My academic training and work have been in analytic philosophy with a focus on practical and applied ethics, while my practical background has been in conflict resolution as a mediator and group facilitator. It was in this confluence of the analytical and the practical that the new *paradigm of empowerment* presented itself to me as a compelling solution in criminal justice.

Throughout the 1990s, restorative justice thinking was relying heavily on a conceptual framework that traded on a false opposition between retributive and restorative justice. From my analytical work on victim empowerment and retribution in the philosophy of punishment (1990–1996) it was clear that restorative justice critiques of the justice system relying on this false dichotomy missed their mark.[3] At the same time, more fine-grained proposals to explain restorative justice, such as Braithwaite's theory of re-integrative shaming, only offered partial, disparate and disjointed accounts of what was happening in practice. Restorative justice was wanting of a plausible over-arching theoretical framework that was philosophically sound and

---

1   Barton 1996 (later published as 1999a).

2   For details on how *the empowerment paradigm* applies to the court processing of offences, see Barton 1996, 1999a (Chapter 10 and Conclusion). See also the exchange with Davis in Davis 2000, 2001 and Barton 2000a, 2002.

3   See Barton 1999a, 1999b. The relevant arguments have also been included here as Chapter 1.

empirically compelling in identifying its essence and thereby guiding its practice and future development.

In my view, the most plausible concept for such a theoretical framework is *empowerment*. Accordingly, I have placed *empowerment* at the centre of my critique and theory of criminal justice, encompassing the conventional as well as the restorative. This decision was supported by two related observations in 1995 while collecting data for the *Re-integrative Shaming Experiment (RISE) Project* in Canberra. Working for RISE afforded me the privilege of observing many group conferences and court cases, as well as the opportunity to interview many of the participants afterwards.

a) There was a striking and consistent *difference* between what appeared to be well run and poorly run restorative justice meetings.

b) There was an equally striking and consistent *similarity* between poorly run restorative justice meetings and court.

To my mind, that difference and similarity were not the presence or absence of retribution as the reigning anti-retributive paradigm of restorative justice in the 1990s implied, and it was not re-integrative/stigmatising shaming which the study was seeking to measure. Rather, it was the individual and collective *empowerment/disempowerment* of the people who were most immediately affected by the crime, namely the victim, the offender, and their respective circles of social support and care. Good meetings, it seemed, consistently *empowered* the main stakeholders, while poor meetings and court consistently *disempowered* them. From what I saw, *disempowerment* had a strong tendency of leaving the affected parties uneasy and unhappy with both the process and the outcome, whereas *empowerment* – whereby the key participants were encouraged to speak their minds and make their own decisions – seemed to make a positive difference, time after time, for all involved.

This simple observation offered itself as a compelling basis for critiquing and re-conceptualising both conventional and restorative criminal justice in terms of a new *paradigm of empowerment,* namely *the individual and collective empowerment of the primary stakeholders in conflict,* that is, the individual and collective empowerment of victims, offenders, and their respective families and circles of social support and care, so that *they* can address the causes and the consequences of the occasioning incident *in ways that are meaningful and right for them.*

While my conclusions on empowerment were at first confirmed in practice by observing group conferences and court cases in Australia, the various second hand accounts that were available to me at the time indicated that the same principle of empowerment was at work in the restorative justice practices of other nations. I have since been able to satisfy myself of this being the case through first hand observations of real life circles and victim-offender mediations. Also, since its first explicit formulations in terms of victim empowerment and victim justice in the early 1990s, I championed the idea through my academic teaching and training, draft papers, seminars, professional conferences, formal and informal discussions with restorative justice practitioners and peers, role play demonstrations, training workshops, and the aforementioned group conferencing manual, which is hereby published in book form. Key elements of the theory were included in my PhD dissertation (1996)[4] and have appeared over the years in a variety of peer-refereed, professional publications, including journal articles, papers, a book, and on the Internet.[5]

Initial reactions to the new paradigm have ranged from the enthusiastic to the cool and sceptical.[6] However, there are increasing signs that restorative justice thinking is abandoning its futile preoccupation with retribution and is slowly embracing instead the idea and language of *empowerment*.[7] To my mind, only the latter can provide a philosophically defensible conceptual framework for good practice and the restorative justice movement.

Unlike most academic publications in restorative justice, this book is as much about good restorative justice practice, as it is about sound restorative justice theory. Rather ambitiously, the book's aim is to equip the reader with a sound understanding of restorative justice theory and good practice, irrespective of the reader's background or interest in restorative responses to conflict, wrongdoing, and crime. Articulation of the theory is in accessible language, and is followed by practical guidelines, suggestions and hands-on techniques that help translate the *empowerment model* into practice. Informed by a variety of styles by practitioners across a range of different programs from Australia and New Zealand to the United Kingdom and the United States, I have tried to crystallise my understanding into a unified and a clear, step-by-step process of restorative meeting facilitation, complete with seating plans and scripted prompts for mediators, keepers, and facilitators. In developing this process, the ultimate consideration throughout has been to enable restorative justice practitioners to achieve maximally restorative outcomes reliably for all participants in their meetings, time after time.

It would be folly to assume that this book could constitute the final word on restorative justice. As restorative justice interventions are being introduced

---

4   Barton 1996, later published as Barton 1999a.
5   Barton 1999a, 1999b, 2000, 2000a, 2000b, 2001, 2002. Barton and van den Broek 1999. See also, "The Empowerment Model of Restorative Justice" on the International Victim-Offender Mediation Association website: <www.voma.org/articles.shtml>.
6   The fiercest resistance appears to be provoked by the idea of substantial and meaningful victim empowerment (Davis 2000, 2001, Barton 2000a, 20002).
7   Braithwaite and Roche, 2001; Braithwaite 2002, 2003; and earlier, Braithwaite and Mugford, 1994. Also, the increasing emphasis on empowerment by Real Justice over the past few years is an encouraging sign. The theme for their latest conference was "Building a Global Alliance for Restorative Practices and Family Empowerment" <www.restorative practices.org>.

in ever more jurisdictions and contexts, what will matter most is how well restorative justice principles are applied in practice. Hopefully, by taking a distinctive stance on what good practice is, this book will prompt reflection and constructive dialogue among practitioners, academics, stakeholders and policy makers on questions of good practice in restorative justice. Even if consensus is never achieved, such dialogue and debate are important to the healthy evolution of restorative justice and the restorative justice movement.

Getting it right in practice requires that mediation and group facilitation approaches be critically examined for their capacity to secure maximally restorative outcomes for all parties concerned. Such examination must have as its primary aim the answering of one crucial question: *Which mediation and facilitation approaches and processes will give us the best results in terms of achieving justice, closure and emotional conciliation for the primary stakeholders, while avoiding victimisation, bullying, and re-victimisation occurring in what are meant to be restorative meetings?*

This is the most important question in restorative justice today. It is also the question that has tended to receive the least attention in the restorative justice literature. Yet, in practice, programs and facilitation processes differ considerably, and practitioners are not immune to believing that they have the best of both, or that their particular approaches are best suited to their local conditions. Having had the privilege of observing practice in a variety of jurisdictions and programs, I could not but conclude otherwise. The isolation of practitioners, the lack of reliable and honest feedback to them on their practice, together with the many sub-optimal processes and approaches I have observed, have given me the incentive to share more widely the essence of what I have understood from observing the many different models that attempt translating restorative justice ideology into practice. Based on those observations and relevant discussions with practitioners, as well as my first hand experience as a practitioner in mediation and conference facilitation, I believe that the empowerment model of mediation, circle keeping, and group conference facilitation is the most powerful to date in terms of reliably capturing principles of alternative conflict resolution in restorative justice contexts.

There is one objection to my enterprise that I should like to dispose of from the outset. This is the claim that there is no single right way of arriving at good restorative justice outcomes. This is true, of course, but also beside the point. For, while even poorly run programs and sub-optimal processes have their share of success, their successes tend to depend more on good luck than design. This is as unnecessary as it is deplorable. What is to the point is the ability of programs and facilitation processes to secure high rates of success reliably across the range of cases entrusted to them from the relatively minor to the most serious.

Sub-optimal mediation and facilitation models and processes will lead to failure in a higher proportion of cases than necessary. While some conferencing programs have consistently recorded high, all-round satisfaction rates among all categories of participants,[8] this is far from universal experience. For example, in the New Zealand Youth Justice Conferences studied by Maxwell and Morris:

a) only in 41 per cent of cases did victims attend the FGC (family group conference) – mostly because they were not invited or were given insufficient notice;

b) of those victims that attended, only in 49 per cent of cases did they express *any* degree of satisfaction with the outcome [my emphasis].

c) only about a third of victims went away from the FGC feeling better;

d) 25 per cent of the interviewed victims said they felt worse as a result of attending the FGC;

e) 38 per cent of FGCs attended by victims who were interviewed resulted in the victim saying they felt worse.[9]

Similarly, with respect to offenders, Maxwell and Morris found that:

a) only a third of young offenders felt involved and often said little in their FGCs;

b) 26 per cent of a sample of 14 to 16 year olds referred to FGCs in 1990–1991 had been (re)convicted within 12 months;

c) 64 per cent of them had been (re)convicted after just over four years;

d) 24 per cent of them had been persistently reconvicted over the same period. (Maxwell and Morris 1997)

Such results are unacceptable.[10] In light of the much-emphasised potential of community involvement in dealing with crime, the above re-offending rates, for example, clearly fall short of legitimate expectations.[11] Also, from a victim justice perspective, some of the above figures are of the gravest concern. Victims of crime have a lot at stake in the way the criminal justice system deals with their cases, and the above rates of re-victimisation raise important

---

8 For example, Moore 1995; Palk et al, 1998; Tuhiwai Smith & Cram 1998.

9 Maxwell and Morris 1993 (p 119); 1996.

10 Poor practice is not reserved to New Zealand. Similarly poor results have been achieved, in my view, in South Australia and the United Kingdom and poor practices of various degrees are present in most programs I have observed around the world. For formal reports on some of the latest findings, see the relevant articles in von Hirsch et al, 2003.

11 Alder and Wundersitz 1994, Barton 1996, 1999a, Braithwaite 1989, 1996; Braithwaite and Mugford 1994; Maxwell and Morris 1993, 1996.

moral and legal questions about the morality and legality of exposing victims to such high risks of re-victimisation in criminal justice interventions.

The challenge to the critics of my project here is to explain the discrepancies between the performance of different programs in terms of factors other than the ones being emphasised in this book concerning good practice. While the New Zealand program may be taking on a higher proportion of difficult and high risk cases than those that show good results, this factor is unlikely to account for the discrepancies on its own. Instead, those poor client satisfaction and re-victimisation figures are in large part due to the continued use of a clearly sub-optimal facilitation process, and the fact that conferences are convened and facilitated by a transient population of conference coordinators. To make matters worse, these coordinators are typically thrown in at the deep end without appropriate training in conflict resolution and conference facilitation techniques. For more than ten years, many coordinators (mostly social workers) have come and gone, using the position of coordinator as a step in their career ladders. All that time, the department responsible for the Youth Justice Conferencing program has failed most coordinators in respect of providing them with appropriate training in conflict resolution and conference-specific facilitation techniques. It is mainly these factors that are responsible for the above results, which stand in stark contrast to results achieved in programs that have adopted better processes, provided varying levels of training to their mediators, keepers and facilitators, and encouraged stability and continuity among practicing staff.

Those who are familiar with the dynamics and intricacies of interpersonal conflict escalation and resolution will recognise that addressing issues such as the above is essential to good practice in any program. Their neglect can only result in disasters, especially in the more difficult, high-risk cases, where victimisation and re-victimisation are most likely to occur. Therefore, it is important to proceed from the premise that there are better and worse ways of preparing and running restorative justice meetings.

An explicitly stated philosophy of empowerment, together with carefully crafted and open-ended scripted prompts to aid the practitioner in his or her task, will consistently deliver the best results achievable. This is what I have attempted to provide in this book.

Charles Barton
Ocean Shores, Australia
September 2003

Acknowledgments

In writing this book I have relied on the support and good will of many individuals and institutions whose contributions is my pleasure to acknowledge. First and foremost, I thank the many program managers, mediators and facilitators in restorative justice, from Australia and New Zealand to the United Kingdom and the United States, who have gone out of their way to allow me observe their practice in face-to-face meetings. This book, which is based so much on my first hand experience of the relative strengths and weaknesses of the various processes and techniques I have observed would not have been possible without their cooperation. Chief among them is Terry O'Connell, to whom I am most deeply indebted for his early mentorship and openness in sharing with me his understanding, ideology, and practical know-how of group conferencing facilitation. His influence on the facilitation process presented here is major and obvious.

I should also like to thank the following institutions for welcoming and hosting me for various lengths of time over the years while working on this project: The Centre for Applied Philosophy and Public Ethics, and the School of Policing Studies at Charles Sturt University; The Centre for Crime Policy and Public Safety in the Key Centre for Ethics, Law, Justice and Governance at Griffith University; the Philosophy Departments at Massey University (NZ) and the University of Colorado at Boulder; and finally, in the UK, the Police in Nottingham, Thames Valley, and Northern Ireland.

INTRODUCTION

Restorative justice meetings and interventions are relatively new approaches to dealing with wrongdoing and crime in the context of the criminal justice system. However, from the early 1990s, governments and communities have been using these processes with increasing frequency in an attempt to find constructive solutions to interpersonal conflict, victimisation, and anti-social behaviour. Through such initiatives, restorative justice interventions have now become significant and recognised tools of Alternative Conflict Resolution both within and outside of criminal justice. Many school communities are now using these methods of dealing with problems, for example, and some organisations use it to resolve conflict in the workplace, as well as to deal with grievances and client complaints. In many places restorative justice meetings are being used to sort out family disagreements and other interpersonal problems.

Some ways of running restorative justice interventions are better than others. Some interventions can be downright disastrous, such as when, instead of having their conflict resolved, people feel silenced, marginalised, disempowered, victimised or re-victimised in their meetings. Typically, this happens when facilitators receive inadequate training and have a less than adequate understanding of the nature, dynamics, and effective management of interpersonal conflict and its resolution. Poor knowledge of effective facilitation techniques leads to poor practice.

The first step towards gaining a sound understanding of restorative justice interventions consists in clearing up the ambiguity in the expression "restorative justice model".

For example, with regard to restorative justice conferencing, a clear distinction must be made between conferencing *program models* and conference *facilitation models*. There are important differences between conferencing programs and the facilitation processes they employ in their interventions and meetings. The distinction between a restorative justice program and the facilitation process(es) it employs must be kept sharply in focus in any discussion or evaluation of a program or so-called "model". Blurring them makes it all the more difficult to identify

1

what works and what doesn't, what needs to be kept and what needs to be changed or improved.

Equally importantly, the distinction corresponds to important spheres of competence and responsibility with regard to good practice in restorative justice. Program features are mostly the responsibility of legislators and administrators of a program, whereas the responsibility of competent facilitation falls, in the first instance, on the shoulders of the practitioners working at the cutting edge, the mediators, convenors, and facilitators of restorative justice meetings.

It is necessary, therefore, to elaborate the distinction between program and facilitation models.

The concept of a *program model* encompasses all the features and elements of the restorative justice program within which specific interventions and meetings are being convened. Such program features and elements include the relevant legislation, the nature of the agency that is responsible for convening meetings, referral and case allocation processes, bureaucratic structures, legislative basis, rights of veto, case management systems and workloads, types of intervention used, the availability of funding to cover travel expenses for participants, organisational guidelines and policies regulating the convening of meetings etc. In this sense of the word, for example, the Wagga model of restorative justice conferencing is different from the New Zealand model – in that conferences in Wagga Wagga were run by the NSW Police Service as police cautions, whereas in New Zealand, Family Group Conferences (FGCs) for young offenders are run by a government department, which is responsible for children, youth and their families, under a conference-specific legislation, the New Zealand *Children, Young Persons, and their Families Act* 1989. Again, what tends to stand out in most people's minds about the Wagga model is that restorative justice meetings in Wagga Wagga were convened by uniformed police officers, whereas meetings in New Zealand are convened by civilian coordinators from a predominantly social work background, who are full-time employees of a civilian government bureaucracy.

While such differences between restorative justice programs may turn out to be significant, I suggest that they are not of primary significance to the key participants in restorative justice meetings, unless such program features seriously impact on the quality of service provided to them. There are far more important factors which affect quality of service to victims, offenders and their immediate communities. Accordingly, I am going to say relatively little in this book about *program models*. Rather, my focus will be on *facilitation models* as defined by fairly specific features of meeting preparation, facilitation, and follow-up. A facilitation model is defined by the particular nature and structure of a meeting – starting from the important question of who gets invited to the various steps and stages in the process, the order in which participants are asked to speak and the kind of contribution participants are prompted to make – and by the specific facilitation techniques the facilitator employs in the meeting, as well as by the kind of follow-up work that is done afterward.

Why focus on facilitation models? In a nutshell, because it is the quality of facilitation which impacts most directly on the key participants. Whether participants find closure and satisfaction in the way the case is handled and the matter resolved depends mostly on the quality of conference preparation, facilitation, and follow-up. If someone is a victim, or an offender, or a supporter for either of them in a conference, what matters most to that person is not whether the facilitator is a police officer, a volunteer, a paid mediator, counsellor, teacher, or a social worker, or whether the broader program is being run by the police, the school, a local community group, or a government department. What matters most to participants is whether the mediator, convenor or facilitator employs a sound and reliable process, whether they have appropriate conflict resolution skills, and whether they use proven techniques of conflict resolution, mediation, and facilitation that maximise the chances of achieving closure and satisfaction with justice for all concerned. In other words, what matters most to the key stakeholders is the quality of the experience from, and following, the meeting. These depend largely on the facilitator's approach and skilfulness in preparing and guiding participants through a constructive process of interpersonal conflict resolution. This is where the particular mediation or facilitation model employed by the program and the skill level of the practitioner make a big difference.

This is not to deny that other features of program models are also important. The various program features can, and do, influence conferencing processes and outcomes.[1] However, reliable program assessment is impossible, unless, and before, we are clear about which preparation, facilitation, and follow-up processes and systems are the

---

1   Appropriate training of practitioners, or a lack of it, are obvious examples. Similarly, work overload results in corner-cutting by practitioners. When this leads to important people not being invited to meetings, high rates of failure and dissatisfaction inevitably follow, especially in cases that are only appropriate for larger group meetings, such as conferences and sentencing circles. I have in mind the more difficult cases where offenders show little or no remorse about their wrongful action, where they have an extensive criminal record and are at high risk of re-offending, for example.

best for the purposes of delivering quality service to clients right where it matters most, at the coal face. Conversely, once we know what is required at the front line of practice, shortcomings and the necessary improvements in the broader program are easily identified.

Moreover, even the best legislation and other positive program features can be undermined and jeopardised by poor facilitation approaches and inappropriate facilitation techniques. These are usually the direct results of inadequate training and feedback systems on quality of practice. Conversely, even unhelpful program features can be ame-liorated and overcome by sound preparation, facilitation and follow-up by practitioners who deal directly with the key participants.

What is a restorative justice meeting?

First and foremost, a restorative justice meeting is a face-to-face encounter between the principal stakeholders. A restorative justice conference, for example, brings together the victim, the offender, and their respective communities of support (family members, friends, col-leagues, neighbours, teachers, coaches, etc) to discuss the wrongful, or offending behaviour in question. The focus is to address the causes and consequences and to find a satisfactory resolution to the incident in ques-tion through consensus decision making.

In contexts unrelated to criminal justice, restorative justice processes can be used as an effective conflict resolution and problem-solving tool. The principles, facilitation techniques and the democratic nature of these processes can be easily transferred to other areas with appropriate modifications. This should be evident throughout the book.

Group conferencing, circles, and mediation: What is the difference?[2]

Group conferencing, circles, and mediation when done well (because all too often they are not) are all democratic, negotiated settlement processes between the principal stakeholders, and all of them may be used as alternatives to, in conjunction with, and in addition to, court. Nevertheless, they are not identical. The most important difference lies in the number of participants that are involved in the negotiated settle-ment of the conflict and the type of facilitation structure employed.

---

2   The views expressed in this section about the similarities and differences between mediation and conferencing are very much from a practical point of view. While more subtle distinctions between the two types of processes may be possible, from the point of view of the practitioner, they are academic.

Mediation takes place mostly between individuals, while conferencing is mostly between communities of individuals because conferencing also includes the principal protagonists' respective communities of support and care. Similarly, circles involve a larger body of participants than the principal parties to the conflict, but they tend to involve more rituals and the flow of communication is typically controlled by use of a ceremonial object, called "the talking piece". Wider group participation tends to make a major difference to the dynamics of the conflict resolution and negotiated settlement process, as does the facilitation process and the prompts used by group conference facilitators and circle keepers. Participants will, by and large, take directions from the person facilitating the meeting, which means that facilitators have a lot of influence on people's participation, and hence on their ability and chances of sorting out all matters to their satisfaction.

An alternative and tempting way of drawing the distinction between mediation and the other two group processes would be to say that mediation deals with civil conflict, whereas conferencing and circles deal with criminal conflict. While this way of drawing the distinction between them reflects their respective contexts of origin, it is not a tenable distinction because both processes have infiltrated each others' contexts of origin. Victim-Offender Mediation Programs are common-place in the criminal justice arena, and conferencing and circle processes have similarly been introduced to deal with non-criminal conflict, and also more generally as a group decision and problem solving tool.

It might be wondered whether one or the other of these processes is better than the others. The simple truth is that all of them have their place. Mediation is cost- and time-effective, and a proven conflict resolution technique. There are many contexts and cases where it is the most appropriate process, such as when the conflict can be easily resolved without the involvement of supporters, and where one or both parties feel that they wish to meet each other without other people being involved on either side. That said, conferencing and circles are more robust and reliable processes than mediation in difficult, conflict-filled and messy cases where there is still a lot of pain, anger, and fear, where there is a high probability of re-offending, where the sincerity of either party is in doubt, and where victimisation or re-victimisation are serious possibilities.

Thus, there are many instances where mediation would be foolish to consider, but where conferencing and circles can deliver good results. Examples are where wrongdoers are severely disengaged, are remorse-less and contemptuous towards their victims, are inclined to play (mind) games, or are unscrupulous in driving "hard bargains" and/or negotiate in bad faith. While in such cases there is very little that mediators can do, facilitators and keepers in group processes can rely on the willing contributions of a strong community of participants to maintain balance and give dominance to the voices of reasonableness throughout the process.

The extra power offered by group processes is perhaps most visible in cases where potentially dishonest negotiators, players of mind games, and drivers of hard bargains are concerned. They are naturally far less likely to indulge themselves and make themselves contemptible in the presence of the most respected and important people in their own lives. This point highlights the importance of inviting the right mix of people in sufficient numbers to restorative justice group meetings.

Who should attend conferences and circles?

In principle, the convenor should invite everybody who has been significantly affected by the offence and anyone who, for some reason or another, is a legitimate stakeholder in the resolution to be reached at the meeting. The facilitator should make a serious effort to invite both the primary victim(s) and the offender(s), as well as supporters for both – preferably not less than four to six supporters on each side, and especially in serious or problematic cases, more. Some of these meetings can have as many as 30 or more participants. Importantly, supporters should be the most significant people in the offender's and the victim's lives, people who they respectively trust and respect. It is the views and expressed feelings of such important and respected persons that stand the most chance of exerting a constructive influence on how the meeting develops and the way matters are dealt with. Victim participation and a strong presence from victim supporters are as important for conferencing success as offender participation and a strong presence from offender supporters. To the detriment of conferencing quality, this is something that many programs and facilitators have not yet learned to appreciate sufficiently to make the requisite effort to create strong participation from both sides. As will be explained later, the effort of creating strong communities on both sides is not merely worthwhile but necessary for eliminating the chances of victimisation and re-victimisation occurring, given that there is always a real possibility for intense disagreements arising between the parties and that emotions will often run high.

What happens at the conference?

Facilitation models vary between programs, and even between individual practitioners. The differences are mostly in terms of who gets invited, the order in which participants are asked to speak, and the kind of contributions participants are prompted to make. There are three main facilitation models contrasted in a later chapter (Chapter 4). For the time being, the following description of what I call the *Empowerment Model* will serve as an example.

Stage I: Exploration

1. Following preliminaries and introductions, the conference is formally opened and the offender is asked if there was anything they wanted to say by way of starting the conference.

2. The offender is prompted to provide a detailed account of what happened, and the way they got involved in committing the offence. They are also encouraged to reflect on the consequences their actions have had on others, including the victim, their own family, friends, immediate community (school, neighbourhood, work place, etc) and themselves.

3. In order to clarify matters of responsibility, the offender is asked outright whether there is any sense in which the incident may be considered to have been the victim's fault.

4. Offender supporters are then asked one-by-one for their views and feelings about the rightness and appropriateness, or otherwise, of what the offender has done, and what they think this means to the victim. They are also asked to say how they have been personally affected by the incident.

5. The victim is then asked to tell what happened from their point of view, expressing their views and feelings about the incident, and explaining the way they have been affected.

6. Victim supporters are asked one-by-one to express their own views about the incident, and explain how the victim and they personally have been affected.

7. Secondary stakeholders (professionals, such as police, social workers, advocates, etc) are given an opportunity to express their views on the matter and raise any concerns that they may have.

8. All participants are asked to say briefly what they have found to be the hardest issues to deal with regarding the incident.

Stage II: Transition

9. The offender is invited to respond to the views and accounts of other stakeholders, especially the victim and their close family and friends. Typically, offenders take this opportunity to express regret over what happened.

10. The victim and relevant others reply to the apologies, or silence, or whatever other response might have been given by the offender.

11. The principal offender's supporters (such as offender's parents and/ or spouse) are given an opportunity to address the victim and the victim's supporters directly if they wish.

12. The victim and relevant others reply to the apologies, silence, or whatever other response might have been given by the principal offender supporters.

Stage III: Agreement

13. The offender and his or her supporters indicate if there is anything they had thought of doing to put things right with the victim.

14. The victim and his or her supporters indicate what *they* would like to see come out of the conference – the kind of outcome that they would consider to be fair and satisfactory. This is also an opportunity for them to respond to any proposals put forward by the offender and his or her principal supporters.

15. The offender is given a chance to respond to suggestions made by the victim and his or her supporters.

16. Other participants, both primary and secondary stakeholders, are given an opportunity for input towards the agreement.

17. An optional private session (caucus) can be held. This opportunity is extended to all stakeholders.

18. In the event of a private session, upon reconvening all participants are given an opportunity to raise and discuss any further issues that may have come up.

19. There is a final opportunity for all participants to express their views on the fairness, or otherwise, of the proposed agreement or outcome. However, final agreement or resolution is a matter between the victim and the offender (and, where applicable, other stakeholders that have a right of vetoing the agreement).

20. The conference is formally closed and participants are thanked for their participation. Key participants are contacted again within a few days to check how they feel about their conferencing experience and whether they have any special needs or suggestions requiring further action.

These stages and steps in the facilitation process will allow every participant to have their say, feel heard and empowered to be part of the decision-making process in working out the conference agreement (where an agreement is appropriate). Its strengths and advantages are spelled out in greater detail in Chapter 4, where it is compared to two other commonly used processes of conference facilitation.

Origins and brief overview of modern day conferencing

In its modern form, restorative justice conferencing originated in New Zealand with the concept of family group conferencing (FGC) under the *New Zealand Children, Young Persons and Their Families Act* 1989. This enlightened piece of legislation was developed in consultation with a wide range of community groups – most notably with Maori communities whose cultural and philosophical influence is reflected in the emphasis placed by the legislation on the involvement of the wider family to take greater responsibility for the offending behaviour of the young person. For the record, there is evidence that various community groups in New Zealand had been using the conferencing process as a way of dealing with problems before the idea was formally enshrined in law.

In New South Wales, the New Zealand FGC model was informed and modified by a decidedly restorative justice philosophy. Most notably, in 1991, Terry O'Connell – a progressive and community oriented police officer in the New South Wales Police Service – developed and formalised for the first time a restorative justice conference facilitation process in the context of a police diversionary program for juvenile offenders, which later became known as the "Wagga model". O'Connell was informed and inspired by favourable accounts of FGCs by Steve Ireland and John MacDonald, who visited New Zealand in 1990. The Wagga model has since been adopted by police in the Australian Capital Territory, the United Kingdom, as well as by various police departments in Canada and the United States – and has been the subject of controversy on account of being a police program. This focus on *who* is doing the conferences, unfortunately, tends to distract people's attention from the restorative potential of the particular facilitation

9

process which was developed by O'Connell. Regardless of the controversy of police involvement in running restorative justice programs, O'Connell's contribution to the evolution of good practice in conference facilitation cannot be overemphasised. Many community groups and organisations around the world have chosen to implement the facilitation model developed by O'Connell. Also, O'Connell's facilitation model continues to be used by training bodies, such as Transformative Justice Australia (TJA) and Real Justice.

Appreciating the history and development of O'Connell's approach to convening a conference will afford the reader a sense of how better facilitation models can be developed and evolved. The initial New Zealand legislation emphasised the importance of holding young offenders accountable for their behaviour in FGCs, and encouraging the wider family to take greater responsibility for addressing the unacceptable behaviour of their young members. In addition to the underlying aim of keeping young offenders out of court, conference outcomes are envisaged by the legislation in terms of material agreements between a number of stakeholders, including the coordinator, the police representative, the offender, and the victim (if present).

While appreciating the stated aims of FGCs, O'Connell sought to go further. Confident that material agreements and other stated aims of FGCs would be more or less automatically achieved, he shifted the emphasis to emotional engagement and conciliation between the parties. He took the view that the ability of key participants to reach a sense of closure depended crucially on enabling them to deal with their emotionality. This focus on emotionality (dealing with hurt, fear and anger etc) was matched with a correspondingly strong emphasis on community involvement on both sides of the conflict.

This author agrees. Involving, creating, and empowering strong communities of support and care around *both* victims and offenders is what good conferencing and other restorative practices are about. The power of strong, caring communities can overcome all obstacles in the path of successful restoration, reconciliation and healing, no matter how serious the case, or how devastating or hopeless a situation may at first appear to be. The popularity and success of O'Connell's facilitation model in a variety of contexts, including the successful resolution of some very serious offences, bear witness to that claim. It has been used with outstanding success to resolve conflict, not only in the area of juvenile offending, but also in dealing with wrongful or otherwise problematic behaviour in families, schools, the workplace, complaints against police, businesses and other organisations, in community corrections, and prisons. It is not accidental that the model has been adopted by so many conferencing programs around the world, including England, Australia, Canada, the United States, and even in the cradle of modern day conferencing, New Zealand.

But, while O'Connell's model stands out as the first clearly articulated facilitation process that systematically focuses on securing closure and emotional conciliation for conference participants, its restorative potential can be further enhanced by means of a few, relatively simple modifications. The same is true, of course, of the first New Zealand conference facilitation model. The need for, and the potential advantages afforded by the modifications and improvements processes proposed in this book can be readily appreciated in light of the theoretical framework developed here, and even more so in light of what we know about the dynamics and social psychology of conflict escalation and resolution in general, and about interpersonal conflict resolution processes, such as mediation, in particular.

The empowerment model of conference facilitation, described in detail in Chapter 2, captures and builds on the strengths of other conference facilitation models developed over the past decade and receives an evaluative comparison alongside the two most widely used models in Chapter 4. The robust design of this process will enable conferencing programs and facilitators to take on the hardest cases with confidence, creating individual and social peace where, to most people, including the parties in conflict, it seems inconceivable. While the philosophical, moral, sociological, educational, social psychological, and human developmental mechanisms through which the restorative justice conferencing process works are yet to be fully explained by the relevant disciplines, significant advances have been made. The most plausible conceptual and theoretical explanations are presented in Chapter 3.

This does not mean that the empowerment model is fail-safe in all respects. As with any other process, agreements may not always be reached, and/or fulfilled. What it means, however, is that, given what we currently know about the nature and dynamics of conflict escalation, management, and resolution, the facilitation process of the empowerment model enables a facilitator to maximise the chances of restoration, emotional conciliation, and closure taking place for the participants, while at the same time providing virtually fail-safe protection for all conference participants against humiliation, victimisation and re-victimisation. Use of the empowerment model, and of its various facilitation techniques and strategies, are strongly, and especially, recommended in high risk and difficult cases.

Such cases are by no means limited to criminal matters. They can present themselves in any kind of disagreement or conflict, and in any context, including schools, the workplace, the neighbourhood, and the family. Amongst the hardest cases to conference, for example, are workplace conferences where there is a power imbalance between the parties as a result of hierarchical management relationships. The dangers of re-victimisation, for instance, are far greater in such cases than in standard, criminal justice cases between offenders and victims who are strangers to one another and who are unlikely to have ongoing inter-action with each other. Paying special attention to such power imba-lances and taking measures to manage the associated risks is, in part, what makes the empowerment model a robust and reliable process in conference facilitation.

The book is divided into two main parts: theory and practice. Part I provides the theoretical foundations for restorative justice in general, and for the empowerment model in particular. Part II provides guidance for putting the empowerment theory of restorative justice into practice. The result is an exposition of both the theory and practice of effective restorative justice conferencing and, by extension (and with appropriate modifications and adaptations), of effective restorative justice processes, including restorative circles and mediation.

PART I

The Theory Behind the Empowerment Model of Restorative Justice

1

A CRITIQUE OF THE PRESENT CRIMINAL JUSTICE SYSTEM

Those who argue in favour of a restorative justice response to criminal behaviour, rather than the present court-based approach, usually do so on the grounds that (1) criminal justice is only (or mainly) interested in retribution, and (2) that retribution and restorative justice are incompatible. The argument runs like this:

1. Traditional court-based approaches to crime (the status quo) are interested only in retribution.

2. The problem with the status quo is precisely that it is retributive.

3. Restorative justice, on the other hand, is non-retributive.

4. Therefore restorative justice is superior to the status quo.

The aim of this chapter is to show that this chain of reasoning in favour of restorative justice misses the mark. To be sure, there are problems with the status quo. But the problem lies not in its retributive character. Rather, the problem is that the status quo *disempowers* the primary stakeholders in the conflict. Typically, it silences and marginalises them. The primary stakeholders are the victim, the offender, and their primary circles/communities of influence and care – typically, their respective families, friends, peers, and colleagues. Their disempowerment is the single most significant reason why the criminal justice system so often fails to achieve justice for those on the receiving end of the criminal justice response, including victims and the general community, who continue to suffer the consequences of the system's inability to prevent re-offending and crime.

Similarly, disempowerment of the primary stakeholders undermines the effectiveness and potential of restorative meetings.

This chapter shows that propositions 1–4, listed above, are false and argues in favour of the following claims:

1. The status quo is not solely interested in retribution.

2. The problem with the status quo is not that it is based on retribution but rather that it disempowers primary stakeholders.

3. Restorative justice is quite compatible with retribution.

4. Restorative justice is superior to the status quo because restorative justice approaches have the potential to empower primary stakeholders to deal with matters the way it is right for *them*.

This chapter has four sections. The first section examines the connection between the status quo and retribution, arguing for claim 1. The second section argues that restorative justice approaches are compatible with retribution (claim 3). The third section argues for claim 2 and shows that the chief weakness of the status quo is the greatest strength of restorative justice interventions. Contrary to the implied suggestion in many restorative justice critiques, the strength of restorative justice responses does not lie in their rejection of punitiveness and retribution, but in the empowerment of communities who are the best placed to address *both* the causes *and* the consequences of the unacceptable behaviour in question. Therefore, to provide restorative justice critiques of the status quo with more bite, this book shifts the focus from punitiveness and retribution to critical questions of *empowerment and disempowerment*. Finally, the last section illustrates how restorative justice can empower those most affected by crime (claim 4).

1. Retribution and the criminal justice system

The claim that the problem with the criminal justice system is that it is retributive is an inaccurate diagnosis, but showing it to be so requires that we understand what is meant by "retribution" and "retributive". There are two senses in which these terms are sometimes used in the philosophical literature: a standard, proper sense and a corrupted sense.

In their proper sense, as indicated in dictionary definitions, these terms refer to the idea that punishment is imposed on a wrongdoer as a matter of just deserts, that they are being punished because they deserve to be. The *just deserts* conception of retribution is defined by reference to a specific type of reason or rationale that is behind the imposition of the punishment, namely the offender's ill-desert, and which is satisfied, through some sort of negative repayment, or pay-back, which is the punishment.

By contrast, in their corrupted sense, 'retribution' and 'retributive' are being used to mean nothing more than 'punishment' and 'punitive,' respectively. This is a corrupted sense for several reasons. First, it ignores the etymology of the word 'retribution,' which is the Latin *'retribuo* = 'I pay you back.' Second, it flies in the face of current dictionary definitions, which are all in terms of the *just deserts* conception already explained. Third, it ignores the vast body of literature on retribution and punishment, which makes a meaningful and important distinction between those two concepts.

This loose and indiscriminate use of the 'retributive' label creates conceptual muddle and linguistic imprecision in an already difficult area. Properly speaking, *punishment* is a much wider notion than *retribution*, as punishment includes not only desert-based punishment (which is the only form of punishment properly called retribution), but also punishment imposed on people for consequentialist reasons such as deterrence, correction, and the rehabilitation of the offender. This latter type of punishment is not retributive, but instrumental, as it is not imposed with the offender's negative moral deserts in mind, but because of the desirable consequences which the punishment is believed, or hoped, to have.

The difference between the two types of reasons for punishment is significant. That difference, in fact, forms the basis of the longstanding debate over the moral acceptability of retributivist *versus* consequentialist justifications of punishment.[1] Therefore, from the point of view of the many scholars already working in this area, it is misleading to characterise just any kind, or form, of punishment as 'retribution' or 'retributive,' regardless of the reasons that underlie its imposition. 'Punishment' and 'punitive' are not synonymous, respectively, with 'retribution' and 'retributive, and the distinction between retributive and instrumental punishment should not be blurred in critiques of the criminal justice system.

Claim 1 – that the status quo is only interested in retribution – can be evaluated in the light of the two interpretations made possible by the distinction between retribution and punishment. Under (a), the *just deserts* interpretation, the problem with the criminal justice system is alleged to be that it is only interested in giving wrongdoers their just deserts. Under (b), the punishment interpretation, the problem with the

---

1   Walgrave (1995), for instance, has a meaningful and active engagement with retributivist and instrumental conceptualisations of the criminal justice system – even though, this chapter argues that retributive interpretations of the system and its objectives are far from compelling.

criminal justice system is claimed to be that it is punitive, and punishment, it is alleged, either doesn't work or it makes things worse.

(a) The problem with the status quo is that it is only interested in giving wrongdoers their just deserts.
There are two major difficulties with this claim. First, even a cursory glance will reveal that the language of criminal legislation is largely instrumental, rather than retributive. Laws are predominantly couched in utilitarian, consequentialist language where deterrence, public safety, the protection of people's rights, and the correction of offenders are the primary reasons and justifications for punishment.

Closely related to this is that sentencing judges rarely justify their sentences with reference to the idea that offenders need to be given their just deserts.

Their foremost considerations are:

- the public interest in safety and deterrence, rehabilitation and correction of offenders;

- the integrity of the criminal justice system in terms of consistency with established precedents; and

- the general principle that, insofar as it is possible, like cases should be treated alike.

Retribution in the "just deserts" sense rarely rates mention as a consideration by sentencing judges, and even when it does, it is hardly the dominant reason for the imposition of the penalty in question.

Perhaps the most telling example of instrumental reasoning being dominant in our courts is provided by *R v Clotworthy* in 1998.[2] This is a fascinating case in which the New Zealand Court of Appeal sent an offender to gaol against the wishes of the primary victim. After discussing the matter with the offender in a restorative justice meeting, the victim considered imprisonment a wasteful and inappropriate way to resolve the matter. Instead, the offender undertook to pay the victim's medical bills by remaining employed. With some modifications, the District Court approved the agreement and the matter was settled to everyone's satisfaction, except the Crown's, who subsequently succeeded in overturning the agreement in the Court of Appeal.[3] The following excerpt contains the main elements of the Justices' reasoning in their decision.

---

2   *R v Clotworthy* (1998) 15 CRNZ 651.
3   For a more detailed description of the case, see Boyack 1999.

We record that Mr Cowan [the victim] was present at the hearing. We gave him the opportunity to address us. He reiterated his previous stance, emphasising his wish to obtain funds for the necessary cosmetic surgery and his view that imprisonment would achieve nothing either for Mr Clotworthy or for himself. We can understand Mr Cowan's stance. He is to be commended for having forgiven Mr Clotworthy and for the sympathetic way he has approached the matter. It must be said, however, that a wider dimension must come into the sentencing exercise than simply the position as between victim and offender. The public interest in consistency, integrity of the criminal justice system and deterrence of others are factors of major importance.[4]

The instrumental nature of the reasoning behind this judgment is clear. There is no mention of the offender having to "pay" for their wrongful action through a harsher punishment, or of the offender's "just deserts" anywhere in the summary of arguments, or in the justification of the decision to impose a three-year custodial sentence. On the contrary, there is much weight given to the need to maintain sentencing consistency in the interests of the public and of the criminal justice system, and the importance of deterring others from committing similar crimes. Interestingly, arguments that Mr Clotworthy was not in danger of re-offending and that he presented no risk to the public by staying out of gaol were accepted by the prosecution and by the court. Notwithstanding, the court concurred with the prosecution that "This was more than moderately serious offending, and the need to deter others for public safety reasons is too important".[5] In view of such consequentialist reasoning by sentencing judges, it is simply not credible to blame retribution for the ills of the court system. To be sure, it can be argued that there are many things wrong with the wisdom of the Justices in the above decision, which will be discussed later in this chapter. Their emphasis of retribution, however, is not one of them.

In light of these considerations, the criticism that the criminal justice system is only interested in giving offenders their just desserts is dubious and can be easily rejected by defenders of the status quo by pointing out that they are doing what they are doing, not for retribution, but for the greater good of society.

(b) The problem with the criminal justice system is that it is punitive and punishment doesn t work or it makes things worse.
This claim also has two main difficulties with it. One is that many people remain convinced that punishment is, or can be, an appropriate response to criminal wrongdoing, especially where serious wrongdoing

---

4   *R v Clotworthy* (1998) 15 CRNZ 651.
5   Ibid.

is concerned. This comes through unambiguously in Umbreit's surveys of crime victims.

> "Without question, nearly all citizens at large and crime victims specifically want criminals to be held accountable through some form of punishment"... Oftentimes, the need for punishment was expressed in terms of "accountability". "Justice to me requires some punishment". "It doesn't have to be severe but has to be something that causes them to know they did something wrong and they have to pay for that".[6]

The second difficulty with the implicit rejection of punishment in the above claim is that it is far more probable that, overall, punishment and its threat play a major role in order maintenance. To be sure, this was the main reason why the prosecution took the *Clotworthy* case to the Court of Appeal, and seemed to be one of the main reasons why the appeal was upheld. One need not agree with the particular judgment reached in that case to appreciate the sense in the reasoning behind it. Even if Mr Clotworthy himself was not in danger of re-offending if given a non-custodial sentence, the need for deterring others from committing similar offences was considered a weighty enough reason to justify a custodial sentence.

More generally, even if the threat of punishment is no longer a deterrent to a relatively small number of repeat offenders, that does not mean that the prospect of punishment, such as imprisonment, for instance, is not a deterrent to the majority of people who otherwise might be more tempted to break the law and violate the rights of others in pursuit of their own goals and narrow interests. At best, the evidence on this point is inconclusive, but the phenomenon of sharp increases in mindless vandalism, looting, and violence by otherwise law abiding citizens when they feel that they can get away with it, should cause us to re-think the wisdom of rejecting punishment altogether.

Also, at a conceptual level, it is far from clear that a criminal justice system is even conceivable (without logical contradiction)[7] if punishment is ruled out as a possible response to criminal offending. A system that manages, controls and responds to crime without resorting to any form of punitiveness may well prove preferable to current practice, but it would be a misnomer to refer to it as a criminal *justice* system. It would be more appropriate to call it a crime *management* system, or a crime *control* system. Where criminal justice is concerned, the concept of justice seems to presuppose the idea of a punitive response, if not that of retribution in its proper, *just deserts* sense.

---

6   Umbreit 1989, pp 52, 54.
7   As in the notion of a married bachelor, for instance.

Such conceptual points, of course, concern the meaning of key terms and of proper language use, which indicate the essential nature of the relevant subject or practice, but will not settle substantive, pragmatic and moral questions, such as whether punishment is a wise or appropriate response to criminal wrongdoing.

To settle such questions conclusively, we would need empirical data of the kind we do not possess. What we do have, however, are established practices, social conventions, and traditions that determine, guide or regulate our responses to criminal wrongdoing on both pragmatic and moral grounds. The acceptability of punitive responses, and indeed the insistence on such responses where the crime is especially abhorrent and great, is a reflection of a deeply entrenched tradition that regards punishment as a fitting, and often necessary, response to serious forms of anti-social behaviour. What makes such responses appropriate is the *retrospective* responsibility mature (and intellectually unimpaired) members of society bear for their behaviour.[8]

This tradition, and the ongoing popular belief that punishment is an appropriate and sometimes necessary response to serious wrongdoing, is reflected in our laws; and indeed in the laws of virtually all known societies and cultures, from the despotic to the democratic – so far so that it is hard for us to even imagine a social order where punitiveness was ruled out as an appropriate response to serious wrongdoing. Therefore, advocates and practitioners of restorative justice should not reject punitive measures, but allow participants to use them within the law as they, through their discussions and negotiations with each other, see appropriate.

2. Retribution and restorative justice

In practice, restorative justice responses incorporate both punitive and retributive measures. Typically, they are mixed with other measures such as increased social and community support to eliminate the underlying causes of the offending, and where indicated, further education and treatment. Indeed, it is difficult to see how restorative justice processes could become a widely accepted, let alone the preferred, response to crime, unless they were either complemented by punitive responses through other forums, such as the courts, or allowed direct incorporation of punitive elements in restorative justice outcomes and resolutions, as in fact they do.

---

8   They bear this responsibility quite independently of the likely consequences of those responses, even though the likely consequences or proposed criminal justice responses should, by all means, be taken into account. (Barton 1999a, Ch 8)

This has been recognised by Judge McElrea, a prominent supporter of restorative justice interventions in response to crime. In connection with conferencing rape cases, he makes the telling point that conference outcomes "might still include imprisonment as part of a sentencing package. Punishment can still play a part in restorative justice without it being the dominating influence it is today". (McElrea, 1996, p 7)

This point should be well taken, especially by advocates of restorative justice. It is important because, unless punitive outcomes are allowed to be part of agreements, the use of alternative conflict resolution processes will never be an accepted practice in criminal justice. This is especially true of those areas where restorative justice responses are needed most: the more serious offence categories where the harm, and the potential for further and ongoing harm, are the greatest.[9] This point also comes through with startling clarity in the documented restorative justice conference between the parents and friends of a murdered young man and his killers.[10]

Once again, it is a mistake to think that punitive elements of an agreement automatically undermine or weaken its restorative potential. Quite the contrary. Some appropriate level and form of punitiveness will enhance the effectiveness of the restorative justice response, and will often have to form part of agreements to be acceptable to the relevant parties. That wrongdoing deserves punishment is a fundamental aspect of our reality, even if that reality is, in part, socially constructed. Our liability to punishment is part of what defines us as mature and responsible members of the moral community and as such cannot be eliminated. As a result, in many cases of serious victimisation, no amount of therapy, or indeed conference discussion, may replace a victim's and the community's need to know that wrongdoing is punished, that justice, including justice in the retributive, *just deserts* sense, is done.

The incorporation of punitive and retributive elements in restorative justice processes, resolutions and outcomes should not cause alarm. The notion that punitiveness and retribution are incompatible with restoration is a myth, and is shown to be so by both history and current practice. Current restorative justice practices have been inspired by, and in many respects modelled on, traditional community-based systems of conflict resolution, which have been well known for their retributive character. A traditional *Maori* meeting that dealt with a rapist murderer, for example, could easily see the man being executed by his own

---

9   Barton 1999a, Ch 9.
10   Dee Cameron: "Facing the Demons", *An Inside Story,* Sydney: Australian Broadcasting Corporation, 1 June 1999.

family as *utu* (repayment), for what he had done, and the retributive character of the Australian Aboriginal practice of spearing the offender as *pay-back* is equally obvious. Claims to the contrary, that such indigenous practices are not really retributive, are but pious misinterpretations of indigenous practices and traditions in matters of wrongdoing and punishment.[11]

Far from having to reject punishment and retribution from the available range of responses, what needs to happen in restorative justice interventions is that any punitive response to wrongdoing is complemented with genuine caring, acceptance and reintegration of the person, as opposed to stigmatising, rejecting or crushing them – provided, that is, that they appreciate the moral gravity of their behaviour and are intent on making amends.

In this way, far from defeating restorative justice, a well pitched punitive measure will form part of, and will enhance restoration for everybody involved. Unfortunately, offenders who are otherwise whole-minded and rational but refuse to respect the rights of others, and choose not to abide by the reasonable norms and laws of civil society, or who, in the context of a restorative justice meeting, treat the victim and other participants with defiance and contempt, leave little or no alternative to punishment and incapacitation.[12]

By failing to recognise and appreciate this point, advocates of restorative justice are hindering their own cause. But they are also creating confusion. Especially because of the mistaken belief that punishment and retribution are incompatible with restoration, some advocates of restorative justice contradict themselves.

For example, Morris and Young assert that retributive justice is "fundamentally at odds with the defining values of restorative justice and cannot, therefore, be part of it", while also believing that "restorative justice ... [does not] remove prisons from available sanctions when parties to the restorative justice process agree to them".[13]

Worse, other advocates of restorative justice tend to give severely distorted interpretations of traditional revenge practices of indigenous people – which, as I have argued elsewhere, are essentially retributive

---

11 Barton 1996, 1999a.

12 But see Braithwaite & Mugford (1994), who have put forward compelling argu-
    ments, not necessarily incompatible with the view I have just expressed, that we
    should never give up making attempts to reintegrate an offender into the
    community of law abiding citizens, no matter how hopeless it may seem at the
    time.

13 Morris and Young 1999, in the sections *Vigilantism* and *Conclusion*, respectively.

in character in the proper sense of that word.[14] The retributive character of these practices tends to be disguised, played down, or outright denied in the restorative justice literature. For instance, Wundersitz and Hetzel identify and describe as "appropriate reparation by the 'offender'" the Australian Aboriginal practice of 'pay-back' which, as they admit, "could include some physical 'reprisal' such as ritual spearing".[15] Consedine goes even further when he explicitly denies the retributive nature of *pay-back* in Aboriginal Australia.

> In all cases we have outlined, while there is so much verbal emphasis on revenge, it is plausible to infer that underlying this is a general aim of achieving order and balance. An injury is done, the status quo is upset, retaliation provides a means by which this may be restored. ... [This] is essentially a restorative process, not a retributive one.[16]

These are confused and misleading interpretations of what, clearly, are retributive practices. The process of *pay-back*, is indeed highly ritualised and is closely monitored and controlled by the community. It is important, however, that the word "ritual" does not mislead the reader. Such "ritual spearing" signifies real spearing, and sometimes multiple spearing of the wrongdoer – often resulting in very serious injuries, and sometimes death.

More to the point, while such *pay-back* is restorative in the sense that it restores social peace between the conflicting parties, and between the wrongdoer and the rest of their community, and while to Aboriginal people it might be less punitive than imprisonment, it is neither credible, nor helpful to describe it as "reparation by the 'offender,'" or worse, to assert that the practice is "not a retributive one". Aboriginal Australians themselves call it "pay-back" and their justification for it is not instrumental in the way Consedine's reinterpretation suggests. Their customary laws, which they refer to as *"The Law"*, require that wrongs *must* be punished through *pay-back*. This is a sacred duty and it is accepted and insisted on by all members of the community, wrong-doers and victims included, as being right on account of *The Law*. And, while it is true that the restoration of social order and social peace are unthinkable without fulfilling the requirements of *The Law* in terms of *pay-back*, the inevitable restorative function of *pay-back* is no ground for a redescription of its basic character as if it were a non-retributive, consequentialist practice.

---

14 Barton 1996, 1999.
15 Wundersitz and Hetzel 1996, p 136.
16 Consedine 1995, p 113.

In light of the above, it is a justified conclusion that restorative justice is quite compatible with retributive justice. The particular degree, form, and mix of retributive, punitive, welfare and other elements in a restorative justice response will, of course, depend on a number of different factors, such as culture, tradition, and circumstance. Positive results from restorative justice programs[17] indicate that concerned communities of care are the best placed to get this mix right, but the point being made here is that positive results are not being obtained through a supposed elimination of punishment and retribution from restorative justice meetings and interventions.

3. Disempowerment in criminal justice

The problem with the status quo is that it disempowers the primary stakeholders in the criminal justice conflict, namely, the victim, the offender, and their respective social circles of support and care which, typically, consist of their respective families, close friends, peers and colleagues.[18] These people are the primary stakeholders in the sense that they have the most to gain or lose by a criminal justice intervention and its outcome. Their empowerment in terms of meeting, discussing and resolving the offence should be sought, not only because they have the most to gain or lose from the intervention, but also because they happen to have the best chance of achieving the following three important objectives that should be pursued in any criminal justice response:

a) preventing re-offending by eliminating the underlying causes of the unacceptable behaviour in question;

---

17 To be fair, empirical data on conferencing success is ambivalent. In terms of participant satisfaction, for example, the results from some programs are nothing short of outstanding, showing near-perfect results. (Moore 1995; Palk et al 1998; Tuhiwai Smith & Cram 1998) In other programs, the results are not as good but, arguably, they are still better, all things considered, than court. (Sherman, et al 1998; Maxwell & Morris 1993; 1996; Maxwell 1998; Morris & Maxwell 1997). There are two likely explanations for the discrepancies between programs. One is that, by comparison, programs with lower satisfaction figures are the ones that tend to take on high risk cases. The other one is that these programs haven't yet addressed some important practice issues, such as adequate and ongoing training for practitioners and quality feedback systems on practice. While currently there is no credible data that would establish the degree to which these factors impact on participant satisfaction in the various programs, it is a clear implication of my analysis here that disempowerment of key stakeholders through poor practice is heavily implicated in sub-optimal results and low satisfaction figures.

18 In another context, Daly points out quite rightly that "The problem in criminal-court practices is not that the female voice is absent, but that certain [gender] relations are presupposed, maintained, and reproduced" (Daly 1989, p 2).

b) reducing and, as far as possible, repair the harmful consequences of the criminal wrongdoing in question, especially the harm caused to the victim;

c) achieving a maximally satisfying resolution or agreement that will meet both the material and the emotional needs of the principal parties concerned. (Retzinger & Scheff 1996) The ultimate aim should be to help the parties achieve closure in terms of emotional conciliation and a feeling that the matter has been dealt with fairly, that justice has been done.

A feeling of satisfaction that justice has been done is difficult to achieve for the primary stakeholders, unless they are empowered to have their say in terms of what they consider to be right and wrong, fair or unfair, and express keenly felt and legitimate emotions of hurt, disappointment and anger in socially acceptable ways. As shown by victim accounts of their experiences of the traditional court system, unless these things can happen, the parties will not feel that they have been heard, or that they and their feelings and views matter in the decision-making process.[19] Also, unless important stakeholders are actively involved in formulating an agreement or resolution, they will be less likely to feel ownership over it, to be committed to honouring it, and to feel satisfied with it.[20] Finally, by comparison to third parties, such as legal and other professionals, primary stakeholders are more likely to know the finer details of the circumstances and the needs of the offender and the victim, and therefore are better able to foresee whether some proposed resolution is going to achieve the above mentioned objectives, and indeed whether the proposed agreement is viable or is more likely than not to set the participants up for further disappointment and failure.

Assuming that the primary function of criminal justice interventions is indeed to promote peace and social harmony by means of ensuring justice for the parties concerned, the suggested diagnosis of the ills of the status quo should be uncontroversial. The criminal justice system, which is epitomised by the traditional court process, is anything but empowering to the primary stakeholders. In their purported mission to protect the innocent and punish the guilty, contemporary criminal justice systems marginalise and disempower the very people who have most at stake in particular criminal justice interventions. Most significantly, victims and accused alike are discouraged and denied real opportunities to take an active role in the legal processing and resolution

---

19 Giuliano 1998.
20 Barton 1999a.

of their cases. In effect, they are reduced to the status of idle bystanders in what, after all, is *their* conflict.

A paradigmatic illustration of what is wrong with the status quo is Sir Anthony Mason's suggestion that the courts could implement restorative justice principles by a coming together of the judge, the prosecutor and the defence lawyer to make a decision as to whether some offender should be given a conference or not.[21] Now, you might ask, what is wrong with that? The simple answer is that it perpetuates the disempowerment of the key stakeholders in this important decision which is likely to make a huge difference in terms of how the case is going to be resolved, which, in turn, has serious implications for the primary stakeholders involved.

This kind of monopoly by legal professionals over important decisions in the criminal justice process is the hallmark of the status quo. The most serious problem with it is that it unnecessarily silences and disempowers the very people who are the best placed to make the decisions in question. Such a system is likely to result in many inappropriate decisions being made, with the result that those who have the most at stake will unnecessarily miss out on the potential benefits of a face-to-face meeting. This is because, apart from being quite often poorly informed, disinterested third parties tend to have their own set of priorities in making such decisions – priorities that are priorities only to them, and which are typical of a bureaucratic state apparatus, and which are often contrary to the more basic and immediate needs and interests of the key parties.

In terms of the empowerment paradigm, the alternative to Sir Anthony Mason's suggestion is obvious. It is the victim and the offender, along with their respective families or communities of support, that should be asked whether they would like to meet face-to-face to discuss and try resolving the matter between them. If they do not wish to have such a meeting, these wishes must also be respected and the case can proceed to court.

In other words, this is where empowerment of the primary stakeholders in criminal justice must start: by giving them the power to choose between alternative ways of resolving the matter. Whether resolution should be attempted by way of court, victim-offender mediation, sentencing circle, or a conference, by a combination of these or by some other method, it should be left to the primary stakeholders to decide. If they cannot reach consensus between them, then the matter can be decided by appropriately qualified professionals, but not before that.

---

21 Opening speech, *Restorative Justice and Civil Society Conference,* Canberra: The Australian National University. February 1999.

Indeed, such general principles of empowerment should be present in all of the major criminal justice agencies: policing, court, and corrections.

Empowerment must be present throughout a restorative justice process. Essentially, the emphasis must be on primary stakeholders being actively involved at all stages and making all the important decisions. And, as long as their proposals, including their proposals for resolution, are within reason and the limits of law, their decisions must be respected and accepted as final. This is the point on which the justices in the *Clotworthy* case fell short. Rather than showing respect to the wishes of the primary stakeholders, and especially those of the victim, they set aside a sensible agreement between the offender and the victim and imposed their own sense of right and wrong – a judgment that left the victim, as well as the offender, deeply unhappy. The victim received significantly less compensation than contained in the initial agreement, as Mr Clotworthy lost his job and became unproductive because of his three-year custodial sentence. Additionally, it cost tax payers $150,000 to keep Mr Clotworthy in gaol, with the likely outcome that he would become more of a danger to the community than he ever was before his incarceration.

Given that the protection of the community from crime was a consideration in the judges' reasoning for their decision, defenders of the status quo must excuse the ordinary citizen for asking the obvious question: Where is the sense in it? Judgments such as this only succeed in supporting calls for a substantial and urgent transfer of power from the professionals of the legal system to the primary stakeholders.[22]

4. Restorative justice and empowerment

It would be naïve to think that all restorative justice interventions are positive and wonderfully successful. All too often they are not. Especially when a program is poorly implemented, without proper training in conflict resolution and facilitation techniques, or with an ill-defined vision and poor understanding of how to implement restorative justice principles in practice, many conferences fail and a significant number of them victimise and re-victimise the key participants. My suggestion is that such unhappy experiences for offenders, victims, and their supporters are the result of silencing and disempowerment, or rather the result of conference coordinators failing to empower them in appropriate ways to speak their minds, and stand up for what they, in good faith, believe to be right and fair.

---

22   McElrea 1996, 1999.

For example, victims can experience marginalisation and severe disempowerment when they:

- are not invited to attend their conferences;

- are given inadequate notice or consideration in setting the time and venue of the meeting;

- attend ill-prepared in terms of having realistic expectations, knowledge of the process, awareness of their rights and responsibilities; or

- attend without a strong group of supporters on whom they can lean if the meeting gets difficult.

In the absence of such safeguards, victims are vulnerable and can feel intimidated and re-victimised, especially if the offender or their family proves hard to deal with. The same holds true for offenders and their families who can find the experience overwhelming and humiliating, unless they are similarly prepared and adequately supported during what is for them a very difficult experience.

The thesis that disempowerment (including the mere lack of empowerment) leads to unsatisfactory results for the key participants in restorative justice interventions can be demonstrated by reference to family group conferences (FGCs). While there tends to be a lot of focus on the successes of FGCs, the reality is that they can fail to achieve justice and closure for the parties concerned in an alarmingly high number of cases. Not only can FGCs fail in terms of reaching agreement between the parties, but they can make things worse for those who have already been victimised through the initial crime. To drive this point home, here are again the victim-related findings from the samples studied by Maxwell and Morris:

- Only in 41 per cent of cases did victims attend the FGC – mostly because they were not invited or were given insufficient notice.

- Of those victims that attended, only in 49 per cent of cases did they express *any* degree of satisfaction with the outcome. (My emphasis)

- Only about a third of victims went away from the FGC feeling better.

- 25 per cent of the interviewed victims said they felt worse as a result of attending the FGC, and

- 38 per cent of FGCs attended by victims who were interviewed resulted in the victim saying they felt worse.[23]

---

23   Maxwell and Morris 1993, p 119; 1996.

To repeat, from a victim justice perspective, such findings ought to be of the gravest concern. Victims of crime have a lot at stake in the way the system deals with their cases, and the above rates of re-victimisation are inexcusable. It is hard to conceive of any moral or legal justification for exposing victims to such high risks of re-victimisation in criminal justice interventions.

The above statistics also underlie the urgency of acting on Braithwaite's observation, that "We need quality research on when and why restorative justice fails".[24] Here then is a clear hypothesis that would be well worth testing through research: *Restorative justice fails in cases where one or more of the primary stakeholders is silenced, marginalised and disempowered in processes that are intended to be restorative. Conversely, restorative justice succeeds in cases where the primary stakeholders can speak their minds without intimidation or fear, and are empowered to take an active role in negotiating a resolution that is acceptable and is right for them.*

Without such all-round empowerment of the primary stakeholders concerned, restorative justice processes will be restorative only in name. They will not succeed in realising the restorative potential of individual and community empowerment, which, in the final analysis, is the fundamental starting point of restorative justice.

This analysis, of course, is at a relatively high level of generality, whereas the devil tends to be in the detail. Therefore, research must focus on the many ways in which empowerment and disempowerment are engendered and experienced in restorative justice processes. All parties must be enabled to negotiate from a position of knowledge, and with confidence that they can deal with this matter and make a positive difference in the outcome.

This, however, requires addressing imbalances of power created by differences in age, gender, culture, social status, institutional affiliation, etc. To give just one more example, unless the conference coordinator is highly skilled in the conduct of multi-party negotiations and conflict resolution, and has a clear understanding of the dynamics of interpersonal conflict escalation and resolution as they relate to the concept of restorative justice in terms of empowerment, they are unlikely to succeed in enabling an already timid or crushed young offender find their voice.

Without the involvement of such a highly skilled coordinator, the young person's experience will most likely be one of continued disengagement, humiliation, victimisation and bullying by adults, who, understandably, will also feel equally frustrated and dissatisfied. By

---

24   Braithwaite 1996, p 24.

contrast, a properly trained and skilled facilitator can prevent such failures in the vast majority of cases by:

- proper preparation of the parties concerned;

- inviting the right mix of supporters in sufficiently large numbers on both sides;

- helping young offenders to find their voice by encouraging them to have first say in the conference (unless this is culturally in-appropriate) to explain and own up to all aspects of what they did, and to accept responsibility for their behaviour voluntarily. Unless this happens from very early on in the conference, an angry victim or a stern police officer can easily, even if inadvertently, knock the last shred of confidence, and/or moral concern for the victim and the rest of society, out of already frightened, timid, disengaged, angry, or defiant young offenders;[25]

- preparing and encouraging victims to have their say and speak their minds as they feel it is right and appropriate in the course of the process. If victims feel discouraged or silenced, or their views, concerns and feelings are discounted even in subtle ways, the chances of re-victimisations become unacceptably high.

Clearly, a high degree of awareness and practitioner competence in effective techniques of mediation and facilitation are crucial for consistently good, all-round satisfying processes and outcomes in restorative justice terms. Without them, restorative justice interventions can only hope to be the kind of dubious, hit and miss affairs reported by Maxwell and Morris.

---

25 The good sense in giving young offenders first say in conferences has been emphasised by Braithwaite and Mugford as early as 1994 (p 150), and by others, such as Patrick Power and myself in conversations with conference administrators and practitioners. The point has also been raised at international conferences, but with no discernible impact on practice. The human dimension seems to dictate that, not unlike the legal professionals they so readily criticise, restorative justice administrators and practitioners are as susceptible as anybody else to seek the comfort of the familiar, and to close their minds too quickly to suggestions and opportunities for improving practice. Therefore, it is very important that good systems and practices are implemented from the very start of a restorative justice program. Unless this is done, changes for the better become increasingly difficult and painful. Even relatively small changes will be met with resistance from within the program by well meaning people who almost invariably equate the concept of good practice with whatever they happen to have become familiar and comfortable with.

2

THE EMPOWERMENT MODEL

The preceding chapter established that the difference between conventional and restorative justice is best articulated, not in terms of the (false) *retributive/restorative* dichotomy that figures so prominently in the restorative justice literature, but in terms of *paradigms of empowerment and disempowerment* of the primary stakeholders (victim, offender and their immediate communities of concern and care) in the criminal justice system's response to the crime.

The primary purpose of this chapter is to articulate the basic concepts and elements of the empowerment model of restorative justice. Empowerment in restorative justice cannot be total empowerment with no limitations. Rather, it must be circumscribed, or *bounded*. The relevant restorative processes and outcomes must be consistent with society's shared and most important standards, norms, and values, not to mention the law. Additionally, restorative justice philosophy emphasises individual and community healing and the creation and re-establishment of social harmony and peace through the criminal justice response to the offence. Thus, the restorative justice empowerment of the primary stakeholders in the resolution of the conflict is not only bounded, but also *directed*.

According to Galaway and Hudson, for example:

> Three elements are fundamental to any restorative justice definition and practice. First, crime is viewed primarily as a conflict between individuals that results in injuries to victims, communities and the offenders themselves, and only secondarily as a violation against the state. Second, the aim of the criminal justice process should be to create peace in communities by reconciling the parties and repairing the injuries caused by the dispute. Third, the criminal justice process should facilitate active participation by victims, offenders, and their communities in order to find solutions to the conflict.[1]

---

1   Galaway and Hudson 1996, p 2.

There is an unstated assumption behind this description that the effectiveness of restorative justice processes rely critically on the *empowerment of the primary stakeholders* in the conflict. Judge FWM McElrea's account of restorative justice makes this critical component more explicit and also emphasises the directed nature of restorative justice empowerment.

> Thus we come at once to the heart of restorative justice, which I define as involving three radical changes to the mainstream western model of justice:
>
> 1) The transfer of power (principally the courts' power) from the state to the community;
> 2) The use of FGC [Family Group Conferences] or some other mechanism to produce a negotiated community response; and
> 3) The involvement of victims as key participants, thereby enabling a healing process to occur.[2]

While a necessity, the directed nature of restorative justice empowerment presents conceptual and practical challenges of its own.[3] Stated briefly, this ideologically driven expectation and commitment to secure "restorative" solutions, and the corresponding working definition of success in terms of "restorative" outcomes, presents restorative justice practitioners with the unenviable task of securing restorative outcomes without manipulation or imposition of a restorative agenda on the parties. The parties often arrive at conciliatory agreements and outcomes without difficulty, but just as often they do not. Forgiveness and reconciliation are the last things on an angry victim's mind, and the self-protective rationalisations of defensive, disengaged offenders are no lesser obstacles.

Restorative justice ideology is one thing – reality often proves to be another. Restorative justice interventions and meetings are often messy, and the road to healing and reconciliation can be rocky, and the path to them, far from being obvious, sometimes may not even be there.

The challenge for the practitioner is to overcome such obstacles by taking the parties through an empowering process of consultation, discussion, venting, and negotiation that will bring them to the point where reconciliation and healing, if these are at all possible in the circumstances, can easily and naturally happen. Trying to manipulate or

---

2   McElrea 1996, p 109.

3   The ideological and practical commitment towards healing and reconciliation also comes through strongly in the restorative justice literature in the form of denunciations of punitiveness and retribution and corresponding exaltations of restoration and reconciliation in response to wrongful and criminal acts. While such a conceptual framework in terms of the (false) retributive/restorative dichotomy is muddle-headed and misleading (Chapter 1), it highlights once again the emphasis placed on restorative justice interventions being helpful and constructive, as opposed to being counter-productive and destructive.

force participants into "restorative" outcomes and agreements not only tends to be counter-productive, but violates people's right to autonomy and self-determination, including their right to hold onto their emotions without fear of disapproval or pressure from outside from people with more power. Thus, in a relevant and very important sense of the word, good restorative justice practice, especially in the more complex and difficult cases, is an art. But, as much as it is an art, it is not a mystery. It depends critically on two major factors:

1. Working knowledge of a sound restorative justice philosophy and of a conceptual framework that operationalises and translates that philosophy into practice.

2. Development and competent application in criminal justice contexts of appropriate skills and techniques of alternative conflict resolution.

The latter of these is addressed in Part II. The present task is to provide a conceptual framework for the former by articulating in greater detail the most fundamental concepts and distinctions that give effect to the idea of *directed empowerment* in restorative justice processes and meetings. Taken in turn, these concepts and distinctions are:

1. Surface versus deep approaches to problem solving.

2. Legalistic versus moral problem framing.

3. Primary versus secondary stakeholders.

4. Individual and community empowerment.

5. The principle of equal justice.

6. The meaning and definition of success in restorative justice practice.

1. Surface and deep approaches to resolving problems

The *surface versus deep* construct signifies fundamental philosophical and ideological differences that are readily recognisable in practice. Within each and every restorative justice program, managers and practitioners have a critical choice between taking a *surface approach* or a *deep approach* to the way their processes and meetings are being run. A *surface approach* is characterised by the focus being on reaching tangible agreements and certain fairly specific material outcomes, such as restitution and compensation to victims, keeping the case out of court, and saving the offender from a criminal conviction and jail.

While such goals and outcomes are important, they do not exhaust, let alone do justice to, the idea of restorative justice in terms of reconciliation and healing. Good practice in restorative justice goes beyond the surface approach, beyond the kind of material externalities mentioned. The fundamental aim and purpose in restorative justice is to bring about closure and healing of the effects of crime, especially the emotional harm, disconnectedness and social isolation experienced by those most seriously affected by the wrongdoing. Invariably, this includes not only the victim and those close to them, but also the offender and their family and friends. Therefore, consistent with restorative justice ideology, good practice is strongly directed towards repairing the damage to individual lives and social bonds by reconciling the parties in conflict and securing a sense of closure for them through the intervention.

Such substantive aims and outcomes (substantive justice) require that practitioners take a *deep approach* in the way they respond to the wrongdoing, its causes, and its consequences. In terms of the process employed (procedural justice) the deep approach means that substantive resolutions and outcomes are achieved through processes that involve *all* the relevant stakeholders, that victims, for example, are not left out. It also means that all participants are empowered and encouraged to speak their minds truthfully and without fear. Finally, it means that participants on both sides are helped and encouraged through appropriate preparation and the skilful use of prompts in their meeting to talk, not only about facts and figures, but also about their emotional experiences of disappointment, anger, devastation and fear. Without dealing with these emotional dimensions of the wrongdoing, closure, reconciliation, and the satisfaction that the matter has been properly resolved and put to rest are unlikely to be achieved.

Indeed, unresolved emotional and moral psychological issues hinder not only healing and lasting reconciliation between the parties, but also material agreements.[4] This reason, however, weighty as it is, is not the main argument supporting the deep approach. Those criminal justice interventions that make the most difference overall to the relevant stakeholders are not only fair and just to the offender in the traditional sense, and they do not merely compensate the victim in material terms; they are also, and principally, restorative in the deeper sense just explained. The deep approach requires a certain kind of focus in the way the criminal justice problem at hand is framed and approached – which leads directly to the next point of discussion.

---

4   Retzinger and Scheff 1996.

2. Legalistic versus moral approaches to framing problems

Program managers and facilitators can choose to treat their cases as primarily *legal* matters, or they can treat them as primarily *moral* matters. In the former instance the problem or incident will be seen as a case where the law has been broken and the main purpose of the intervention is to determine the most appropriate response to the offence which is understood and treated primarily as *a violation of the law.* This kind of interpretation of the offence leads more or less automatically to a surface approach in terms of both the process and the kind of resolution sought. This is so because the focus is on the law and formal requirements in terms of achieving material agreements and resolutions, rather than the *moral violation* of particular individuals and communities whose lives have been wrongfully disrupted by the wrongdoer and who, as a consequence, are likely to feel deeply violated, upset and angry. Such social and moral psychological considerations, and participants' corresponding needs in terms of closure, conciliation, and emotional healing, are more naturally the domains of *moral* problem framing.

The likelihood of legal framing is particularly high in cases where legal professionals step into power vacuums created by poor facilitation processes, or by poor preparation that results in low attendance rates from primary stakeholders.

Consider some typical examples.

Suppose that the victim fails to attend. They may or may not be represented by professional people from a victim support organisation. Or suppose that the victim attends the meeting but does not feel empowered enough to participate confidently because of poor preparation or facilitation in the meeting, or because they feel intimidated in the absence of support from family and friends who were not invited or encouraged to attend. Suppose also that there is a similar lack of support and empowerment for the offender, and that this is compensated for by the attendance of a legal advocate. In such meetings it is almost inevitable that the legal advocate and the police officer, or even a victim advocate, or a social worker, will dominate the discussion, possibly speaking "legalese", quoting statutes, current court practice and precedents, trying their best to clinch what they consider to be the best deal for their respective clients. Indeed, in the absence of powerful communities of support and care for both the offender and the victim, it is hard to see how else a meeting like this could proceed.

While such processes may be more interesting and action filled for the relevant professionals, they seriously short change primary stakeholders. They are but a recreation of the court room (bar the judge) with all the characteristics of a surface approach. It is important, therefore, that facilitators do not allow restorative justice interventions and meetings to go down this track. Consistent with restorative justice philosophy, the alternative is to frame and conceptualise offences as *moral wrongs* that have been committed against specific, identifiable individuals. In other words, when an offender is confronted in a restorative justice meeting, they should not merely, or primarily, be facing a legal issue of having broken the law. Rather, they must be confronted with distinctively moral issues of right and wrong, especially in terms of the harmful consequences their actions have had on others.

Questions of how best to repair the harm caused, and of how to put things right, are also moral matters. Principally, it is a moral expectation that offenders should make appropriate amends for their wrongful behaviour, that they should put right the wrongs they committed. Thus, to the extent that participants in a restorative justice meeting discuss the criminal behaviour in question by focusing on its moral and emotional dimensions, they engage each other as members of the moral community, as real people with hopes, dreams, fears, and vulnerabilities. This kind of moral and emotional engagement with each other is much more meaningful and satisfying to stakeholders than the dry, bureaucratic and legalistic approach of the professionals who have no personal or emotional investment in the matter and its resolution.

This is not to suggest that professionals should not be involved in these matters, nor that they should make an emotional investment in them, but rather that secondary stakeholders, professionals and other third party participants need to be aware and must respect the emotional and moral psychological needs of the primary stakeholders for restoration in terms of closure, emotional conciliation, and healing. In practice this means that professionals at the very least take the back seat in restorative justice meetings, and allow the community of primary stakeholders to deal with their issues and emotionality as *moral* matters, rather than as legal matters to be resolved through an adversarial process. Ideally, their role is to provide appropriate information and support for primary stakeholders, thus maximising, in restorative justice terms, the benefits of the meeting for everyone involved.

While professionals must discharge their respective roles and responsibilities to the parties, the law, and the public interest, they must do so in ways that do not marginalise, disempower, or otherwise interfere with the emotional healing and reconciliation which is so important to primary stake holders. They must resist the temptation to dominate the meeting by focusing on legal and other technicalities that are of interest mostly to them, or by behaving as if they were supposed to be the major players and decision makers in the matter. They are not, and if they are allowed to be, then restorative justice meetings are hardly worth the trouble. From the point of view of marginalised and disempowered participants, the case could just as well have been left to the courts.[5] Alternatively, it could have been disposed of as a police caution, which would be much cheaper, less time consuming and all round less troublesome and aggravating for everybody involved.

3. Primary and secondary stakeholders

Ideally, in a restorative justice meeting there is restoration and healing for all key participants: the victim, the offender, and their respective communities of support and care – which typically consist of family members, close friends, colleagues and neighbours, trusted and respected teachers, coaches, counsellors, members of one's church etc. For the sake of conceptual clarity and good practice it is important to think of all these participants as being *the primary stakeholders* in the case and to think of facilitators, social workers, psychologists, lawyers, police, etc, as being *secondary stakeholders*.

While not all stakeholders fall neatly into one or the other of these categories, the *primary versus secondary* construct signifies fundamental differences between different types of participants, which will be reflected in good practice. As we have seen, restorative justice conceptualises crime primarily as a social, or rather anti-social, exchange between individuals that results in injuries to specific people and communities, rather than to "The Law", "The Crown", "The People", or "The Queen". Wrongdoing and crime are committed by one person, the wrongdoer or offender, against an identifiable other, the victim. Especially when there is an identifiable victim who has been wronged and harmed, it is a distortion and obfuscation of the truth to claim that the crime was committed against the state.[6]

Starting from such a fundamentally different theoretical position from traditional criminal law theory, restorative justice philosophy also holds that, as long as agreements are within the law and do not obviously harm the public interest, resolutions reached between the parties are primarily *their* business, not that of professionals representing the state. Unlike the offender, the victim and their respective families and friends, professionals do not have, or at least they are not

---

5   However, acquiring a criminal record would still remain a relevant and important consideration where court would be the only alternative to a poorly run meeting.

6   For a more complete argument on this point, see Barton 2000a.

supposed to have, anything major or personal at stake in the way the matter is resolved. Since it is the primary stakeholders who are most affected by the wrongful behaviour in question, the primary focus of a criminal justice intervention ought to be their restoration and healing, and the efforts of the professionals must be directed toward this end.

When there is closure, emotional conciliation and healing between the primary parties, reaching concrete agreements and tangible outcomes between them also becomes easy, if not automatic. Conversely, even if tangible agreements and outcomes are reached in terms of the surface approach, but the process fails to achieve closure, emotional conciliation and healing for the primary stakeholders, the proclaimed success of the intervention will be overshadowed by a serious failure in restorative justice terms. When this happens, not only is there no sense of closure and satisfaction for the primary parties that justice has been done, but the likelihood of the offender reoffending remains unaffected. Additionally, there is an increased likelihood that some primary stakeholders are left with a sense of having been victimised or revictimised by the intervention or the meeting. Therefore, maintenance of a clear distinction between primary and secondary stakeholders in restorative justice is critical.

As to the responsibility for ensuring constructive participation in restorative justice processes and meetings by professionals, that lies squarely with the facilitator. The facilitator can ensure that their participation is constructive by:

- informing professionals beforehand of what is expected of them;

- involving them only at appropriate stages of the process or the meeting;

- helping them to stay within their roles through appropriate prompts and facilitation techniques, such as asking them the right questions at the right time and, when necessary, asking them to express their concerns at a later point when so prompted (by the facilitator).

These points highlight once again the importance of competent practitioner training – a subject that will be discussed in more detail below. They also highlight the importance of inviting sufficient numbers of supporters of the right kind for both the victim and the offender. In the face of a strong group of supporters, the need, the temptation, as well as the ability of professionals to take over will diminish – which leads to the next critical consideration, the importance of creating and strengthening communities of support and care on both sides of a criminal justice conflict.

4. Individual and community empowerment

(a) Invitation and involvement

Quite often, achieving closure and emotional conciliation through restorative justice processes depends critically, not only on individual, but also on community empowerment. Especially in the more serious and difficult cases, the power of restorative justice consists in the creation and empowerment of a community of caring supporters for both the victim and the offender. Their supporters should be the most significant people in their respective lives, people whom they trust and respect most at a personal level, people with whom they have, or have had in the past, significant personal and emotional ties. Typically, these will be family members, friends, colleagues, neighbours, teachers, coaches etc. There should not be less than four to six such supporters present on each side. As a general rule, however, the facilitator or convenor should invite everybody who has been significantly affected by the incident and anyone who is a legitimate stakeholder in the resolution that may be reached at the meeting. Some of the most powerful and successful restorative justice meetings have had 30 or more participants.

Balanced and empowered communities of supporters are a facilitator's greatest asset. They are the foundation of consistent success, and a most reliable measure against people feeling victimised and revictimised in meetings when things get difficult, as they often do. By tapping their support for the offender and the victim at appropriate times, and by prompting for their views and judgments on crucial matters of right and wrong, harm, responsibility, punishment, apology, forgiveness, reparation and conciliation, a facilitator creates an atmosphere of safety, reasonableness and trust in which even the most difficult issues can be discussed and dealt with in a fair and sensible manner.

By contrast, the absence of either the victim or the offender, and poor supporter presence tends to generate all kinds of problems and difficulties. In such meetings facilitators need to work hard to keep things on track, and it tends to be under such conditions that they abandon neutrality and impartiality in an attempt to balance and rescue a deteriorating situation. This should never happen. Moralising, patronising, and intimidating behaviour by a facilitator are not only wrong, but also unnecessary when there are sufficient numbers of victim and offender supporters to draw on for correcting and balancing skewed perspectives, and cooling and stabilising heated and volatile situations in the course of the meeting.

(b) Empowerment

Once invited and involved, individuals and their supporters must be empowered so that they, as a community, can deal with both the causes and the consequences of the incident in question. The degree to which this can happen depends critically on the extent to which professionals let go of their own institutionally sanctioned power and control. Provided that proposals are within the law and are not unreasonable, professionals must share and use their power to support the primary stakeholders in dealing with their own issues and problems the way it makes sense and is right for them. Local problems are often best addressed through local solutions. In most cases it is the primary stakeholders who are best placed to decide how best to address, not only the consequences, but also the causes of the wrongful behaviour in question, thus minimising the chances of their recurrence.

In practice, individual and community empowerment requires that primary stakeholders be adequately informed beforehand of their decision-making powers, and of their rights and responsibilities in relation to the case. They must know and must be reassured that *they* can deal with these issues, and that competent professionals will be there to help them. Next, in the actual meeting they must be enabled and encouraged to express their views and feelings concerning the matter at appropriate times and stages in a well designed process. Primary stakeholders must not be ignored, sidelined, silenced, trivialised, or intimidated, either by secondary stakeholders, or by other primary stakeholders who may be more vocal and dominant. Finally, crucial decisions in terms of outcomes and resolutions must be made through consensus decision making by primary stakeholders, if necessary through the help and support of professionals and other secondary stakeholders present.

Provided that sufficient numbers of primary stakeholders are present at the meeting from both sides, it is not the place of secondary stakeholders to veto a resolution with which all primary stakeholders are happy and satisfied. The primary stakeholders must not be disempowered by professionals. If they are sidelined, or are being dictated to, there is little point in their attending the meeting; they may well have been better off without it.

(c) Two concepts of a community

The concept of community empowerment in restorative justice is not as precise as it may at first appear, or as we need it to be. It can mean the *community of primary stakeholders* in the conflict, that is, the offender, the victim, and their respective families, friends, trusted neighbours, colleagues, etc. Alternatively, community may be taken to mean a *community of secondary stakeholders* who represent the wider community, such as selected and trained community representatives, and other professionals, such as the police, probation officers, social workers etc. In practice most restorative justice programs create a mixed community of participants from both categories.

However, the transfer of the state's power referred to by Judge McElrea is incomplete if the power currently invested in the courts and criminal justice professionals is transferred only, or mostly, to other *secondary stakeholders* in the conflict, especially since many of them are still the state's representatives.

Decision-making powers – in terms of determining eligibility for diversion from the courts and in terms of the final resolutions reached in each case – should predominantly lie with the community of primary stakeholders, rather than with secondary stakeholders. Since restoration and healing are mostly needed in the community of primary stakeholders, it is *they* who need to be mostly involved and empowered to deal with the causes and consequences of the incident or conflict in question. When a meeting is dominated by secondary stakeholders, primary stakeholders will feel marginalised and the restorative, peace making, and healing potential of the meeting is undermined.

Overly vocal and dominant secondary stakeholders can also inhibit the degree to which primary stakeholders will express their thoughts and feelings about the incident. For example, when an offender musters the strength to talk about their feelings of shame at having betrayed the trust of loved ones, it is most unhelpful of a secondary stakeholder to cut them short in pursuit of a different agenda. Ultimately, it is the facilitator's role to ensure that secondary stakeholders do not inhibit active participation and self-disclosure from the primary stakeholders. To the extent that meetings are characterised by such inhibiting factors of individual and community empowerment, they will fall short of their potential in restorative justice terms.

5. The principle of equal justice

Focusing on restoration and healing also highlights the importance of taking seriously a hitherto neglected side of criminal justice: *criminal victim justice*. The experience of victims in the standard criminal justice process is captured well by Judith Simpson's one line summary of an edited collection of survival stories by victims of crime:

As you will note, in every story the victim is revictimised by the system.[7]

Restorative justice is meant to be different. In view of the emotional harm, disruption, and social isolation experienced by many victims as a consequence of their victimisation, securing for them a fair and just process is as imperative as it is for the offender. If they are to be consistent and successful, restorative justice programs and interventions must give effect to the notion that crime is primarily a matter between the victim and the offender, rather than the offender and the state. Restorative justice ideology is explicitly predicated on the principle of equal justice, that *justice and fair treatment are equally the right of both the victim and the offender*. While traditional criminal justice systems are quick to pay lip service to the principle, their processes and procedures almost invariably disempower and revictimise the victim.

Unfortunately, victim interests continue to figure as secondary even in what are meant to be restorative justice programs. For example, in the samples studied by Maxwell and Morris:

> Victims actually attended in less than half the cases when they could have been present. This failure of victims to attend ... was largely due to poor social work practice. Only 6 percent of victims said that they did not want to meet the offender. When invited at a suitable time and with adequate notice, victims attended.[8]

A victim attendance rate of less than 50 per cent is unacceptable from a restorative justice point of view. Data from the Reintegrative Shaming Experiment (RISE) Project indicates that in Canberra victims attended 86 per cent of conferences.[9] Even this figure is too low. The Wagga Wagga Police conferencing program in NSW has shown that with skill and dedication a near-perfect (98%) victim attendance rate is achievable.[10]

While victims who are uninformed and are not encouraged to attend miss out on opportunities for restoration and healing, it must not be assumed that restorative justice interventions and meetings will automatically result in restoration and healing for attending victims. Maxwell and Morris found that among victims who did attend their conferences only in 49 per cent of cases did they express any degree of satisfaction with the outcome; only about a third of victims went away

---

7   Personal correspondence with Victims of Crime Assistance League (VOCAL ACT) Administrator, Judith Simpson. The book referred to is Giuliano 1998.

8   Maxwell & Morris 1996, p 99.

9   Sherman et al 1997.

10   Moore 1995.

from the FGC feeling better; and about a third of them said they felt worse as a result of attending the FGC.[11]

On the basis of such figures, Maxwell and Morris concluded that "as a system of restorative justice, family group conferences are not always successful".[12] This is an understatement. From the point of view of victim justice and victim restoration such results are unacceptable. They raise important ethical and legal questions about exposing victims to such high risks of revictimisation.[13]

6. Success and failure in restorative justice

(a) Restoration and closure

Restoration for primary stakeholders – in terms of reported and visible signs of closure, satisfaction, emotional conciliation and healing – is directly related to the facilitator's competence in preparing and running a restorative justice meeting consistent with the deep approach, previously described. Conversely, participant dissatisfaction, experiences of victimisation and revictimisation are largely related to poor practice which is all too clearly linked to inadequate training and the lack of ongoing quality feedback on practice. Good initial training and ongoing feedback are essential to evolving, refining, and maintaining good practice.[14] The onus is on those entrusted with the implementation and the running of restorative justice programs to establish good practice in their jurisdictions by ensuring that all facilitators receive appropriate training, and that nobody is allowed to practice until they can demonstrate minimum standards of competency in meeting preparation and facilitation.

The program studied by Maxwell and Morris is a very good example of how *not* to implement restorative justice programs. The poor client satisfaction and revictimisation figures are mainly due to the continued use of a sub-optimal facilitation process,[15] and the fact that

---

11 Maxwell and Morris 1993, 1996.

12 Maxwell & Morris 1996, p 100.

13 Barton 1999b.

14 Maxwell & Morris 1996, p 103.

15 For example, apart from poor victim presence and the near-complete absence of communities of support for the victims, for the most part conferences also fail to create strong communities of support for the young offender who, perhaps, would need it most. Additionally, not unlike in the court room, meetings almost invariably start off with the police officer reading out the charges, followed by the victim's account, with the young offender having the chance to speak only after that. This is a back-to-front process and is disempowering and intimidating, especially to an already timid and fearful young offender. The good sense in giving young offenders first say in restorative justice meetings has been emphasised by Braithwaite and Mugford as early as 1994 (p 150), and later by others, but with little effect. (Barton 1999b, as published in Strang and Braithwaite.)

meetings are convened and facilitated by a transient population of coordinators. To make matters worse, the coordinators were typically without appropriate training in conflict resolution and facilitation techniques. For well over a decade, many coordinators (mostly social workers) have come and gone, using the position of coordinator as a step in their career ladder. All that time, the department responsible for the program has failed to provide appropriate training in conflict resolution and conference-specific facilitation techniques to its practitioners.

Such program implementation and practice, it could be argued, is not only substandard, but reprehensible.[16] There is a serious obligation on everybody involved in the planning and implementation of restorative justice programs – from policy advisers and legislators to program managers and facilitators – to ensure that restorative justice interventions make a positive difference for the primary stakeholders. At the very least they should not end up worse off than they were before, or would have been without, that intervention. Moral duty to the primary stakeholders, and the moral responsibilities of public office require that no criminal justice program is allowed to deliver below this minimum.

Moreover, it is important that poor results such as the above and those reported by Daley from South Australia[17] are not accepted as a given (as if this was the best that restorative justice can do), or worse, discounted or played down. Poor findings should not lead to a lowering of standards and expectations through redefinitions of success and failure in terms of the lowest common denominator. This conflicts with Maxwell and Morris who say that:

> the real measure of the success of family group conferences is the extent to which they represent a fair, humane and acceptable method of dealing with young offenders.[18]

From the point of view of restorative justice this is clearly setting the standard too low. Restorative justice interventions must deliver more than merely being "a fair, humane and acceptable method of dealing with young offenders," for, arguably, so is court. Rather, the question to ask is: *What kind of difference can restorative justice interventions make that are not possible through court?* According to restorative justice ideology and philosophy, the difference must be in terms of achieving closure,

---

16   The lack of inadequate training has been pointed out in a Ministerial Review as early as 1992, and subsequently by Maxwell and Morris (1993, 1996). In terms of providing practitioners with training in conference-specific facilitation and conflict resolution techniques, there has been little change.

17   Daley 2003.

18   Maxwell & Morris 1996, p 105.

emotional conciliation, and healing for all primary stakeholders in line with the deep approach.[19] Also, such criteria of success in restorative justice must be defined by reference to *both* offender- and victim-focused criteria. We must not allow discounting their importance by defining "real" success in terms of weaker, less demanding criteria – criteria that do not even reflect any of the distinctive features and elements of restorative justice ideology. Rather, deficiencies in practice should be highlighted so that they may be rectified in light of standards that are clearly based on restorative justice ideology and philosophy.

(b) Recidivism

While not unique to restorative justice, the challenge of combating persistent offending is an important criterion of success by which the effectiveness of restorative justice interventions must be measured. It is not at all unreasonable to expect that restorative justice interventions will show themselves to be more efficient than court at combating recidivism, especially in the most difficult cases. Naturally, the more difficult a case and the greater the need for social reintegration and community support, the better the preparation, the program support, and the actual facilitation of the meeting must be. Otherwise, restorative justice interventions will have no better chance than traditional criminal justice responses in addressing the underlying causes of persistent offending.

This is clearly borne out in the aforementioned program where only a third of young offenders felt involved and often said little in their FGCs: 26 per cent of a sample of 14–16 year olds dealt with through FGCs in 1990 – 91 had been (re)convicted within 12 months, 64 per cent of them had been (re)convicted after just over four years, and 24 per cent of them had been persistently reconvicted over the same period.[20] These results are more than disappointing. In light of the much-emphasised potential of community involvement in dealing with crime, the above reoffending rates clearly fall short of legitimate expectations.[21]

---

19 Judged only in these terms, in my view the program in question falls well short of its restorative potential. The fact that many young offenders are diverted through it from court could be considered a benefit that, arguably, is not due to the program being "restorative" in intent or nature. By definition, any sort of diversionary program will have the effect of reducing court appearances.

20 Morris and Maxwell 1997.

21 Alder and Wundersitz 1994; Barton 1999a; Braithwaite 1989, 1996; Braithwaite and Mugford 1994; Consedine 1995; Consedine and Bowen, 1999; Maxwell and Morris 1993, 1996; McElrea 1993, 1996; Moore 1993; O'Connell 1996, 1997. Umbreit 1989; van Ness 1990; Wright 1996; Zehr 1990.

To conclude, in cases where restorative justice interventions fail to reduce persistent offending, we must first examine whether the quality of preparation, facilitation, and program support are up to standard. It would be premature to dismiss restorative justice in the high risk cases before we even satisfied ourselves that the relevant attempts had been by well-trained facilitators. Such facilitators would use the deep approach rather than a surface approach, frame problems in moral rather than legal terms and observe the principle of equal justice between offenders and victims. Just as importantly, they would give practical significance to the distinction between primary and secondary stakeholders in the resolution of the conflict by empowering the former and ensuring that backup support is provided by the latter.[22]

---

22   The latest research on FGCs and reoffending by Maxwell (1998) confirms these hypotheses. A more detailed explanation of *how* restorative justice interventions can put an end to persistent offending has been argued by von Willigenburg (1996) and Barton (2000b). Those arguments are repeated here in Chapter 3.

3

WHAT WORKS: SOCIAL AND MORAL PSYCHOLOGICAL MECHANISMS IN RESTORATIVE JUSTICE

According to traditional wisdom, the just and fair (or the most appropriate) response to a criminal act is best determined by criminal justice professionals. The main deficiencies of this approach are as follows.

1. Professionals, no matter how competent they may be in their respective fields, typically do not possess the detailed knowledge and appreciation required for addressing successfully the specific justice (and welfare) needs of the principal parties (victim and offender) in the criminal justice conflict. Only the parties themselves and their close communities of care (typically family members and friends) have the requisite detailed knowledge of their personal needs and circumstances to come up with truly constructive and adequate responses and solutions to the criminal incident, its causes, and its many consequences.

2. Criminal justice professionals and bureaucrats inevitably operate with bureaucratic and procedural priorities that usually fail to reflect the justice needs of the primary stakeholders involved. As a result, outcomes and resolutions imposed by professionals tend to prove unhelpful, or even counterproductive, for the people who are already in considerable or serious trouble and distress, and who have the most to lose or gain by the criminal justice response.

3. The parties feel no ownership over responses and outcomes that are decided, and are forced on them, by others. Consequently, even wise and competent decisions by professionals will tend to result in less

stakeholder satisfaction (probably unfairly) than they would have if they were arrived at freely by the parties themselves in negotiation with one another.

4. Traditional processes of the criminal justice system disempower both parties in the conflict and create a sense of isolation and unnecessary alienation between them, thus exacerbating feelings of helplessness, anger, hatred and fear, which in turn worsen the plight of everyone involved on both sides.

5. Arising from an antiquated criminal justice theory, traditional criminal justice processes fail to acknowledge that seriously wrongful and criminal acts are primarily a violation of specific people, namely the victims of crime (where there are identifiable victims), not the state, or "The Law", "The Crown", "The Queen" or "The People". Therefore it is the victim who is the primary and most legitimate claimant against the offender in a criminal justice response.[1] The subrogation of the victim with such abstractions in criminal justice is increasingly recognised as indefensible, and traditional criminal justice systems have responded to victim justice issues with too little too late.[2]

While defending these reasons falls beyond the scope of this chapter, the rapid proliferation of restorative justice interventions around the world in the past decade has been principally due to them.

In restorative justice interventions the critical decisions of a criminal justice response (concerning justice, prevention, and welfare) are made by the principal parties (victim and offender) themselves, in dialogue with one another and ideally with the support of their respective communities of care. Such interventions are appropriate wherever there is an identifiable victim and responsibility for the offence is not in dispute, and both parties are willing to meet in an attempt to settle the matter through a process of discussion and negotiation. It is only when one or more of these conditions are not met, or where no mutually satisfactory agreement between the parties can be reached, that a case should be dealt with through traditional processes of the criminal justice system.

Why do restorative justice interventions work the way they do? Answering this question will help us understand better why conventional responses to crime have little chance of doing any better than they have already done. This chapter outlines four theories of what

---

1   For a more complete argument on this point, see Barton 2000.

2   These responses have tended to be in the form of victim-specific legislation and Victim Impact Statements, both falling substantially short of meeting legitimate victim needs and interests in the system's response to the offence. (Barton 1999a)

takes place during well-run conferences. The four theories describe various individual, social and moral psychological mechanisms, based on the following concepts:

- reversal of moral disengagement;

- social and moral development;

- emotional healing;

- reintegrative shaming.

Reversal of moral disengagement

This is a moral psychological theory proposed by this author as to what occurs during successful restorative justice conferencing. It starts with the observation that when someone engages in activities which are harmful to others, they will tend to silence their conscience by means of various internal mechanisms of moral disengagement. In a different context, Albert Bandura identifies four such mechanisms of disengagement.[3]

a) Rationalisations about good consequences which are imagined to outweigh the bad ones (moral justification). ("If I make enough money on this, I can later help others.")

b) Obscuring or otherwise lessening personal responsibility for the wrongful activity. ("It wasn't my fault. I just did what I was told"; "I played only a small part in it"; "Others do it, why can't I?")

c) Denial of the seriousness of the harmful effects on others. ("They won't mind"; "They will be fine"; "It's only a few bits and pieces (TV, stereo, jewellery, etc) and they can afford it or claim it on insurance.")

d) Blaming, dehumanising, or otherwise derogating the victim. ("Foolish folk. Should not have left the window open"; "Stupid man. He tried to be a hero"; "He was a bastard"; "She was a bitch"; "Serves them right. They should (not) have ...")

These concepts are highly relevant to explaining the transformative power of well run restorative justice meetings. When victims tell offenders face-to-face about the harm the offenders' actions have caused, offenders' internal mechanisms of disengagement are seriously challenged and, in most cases, reversed. Suppose, for example, that the

---

3   Bandura 1990.

offender has committed a burglary and has disengaged his conscience by the kind of derogation of the victim described in (d). He tells himself the victim is "a selfish rich bastard who deserves what he got and who won't even feel the loss". By meeting the victim, and hearing the victim's point of view, this disengaged stance can be undermined and even reversed. Such reversals of moral disengagement are important in criminal justice, not only for successful offender reintegration, but also from the point of view of victim restoration. They form part of the healing experienced by victims because, as restorative justice experience shows, the sight of disengaged and unmoved offenders is aggravating and distressing to victims – even though good facilitation practice can overcome even this impediment in the path of successful victim restoration and healing.

However, offenders are not the only ones who morally disengage following a criminal offence. There are good reasons to believe that similar mechanisms of moral disengagement often operate for victims and their supporters as well. Moral disengagement may be a significant factor in the resentment which the victim may feel toward the offender. Victims may disengage from offenders by demonising them in statements or thoughts such as "He should be hanged"; "He is a monster"; "He is an animal, not a human being." However, as with disengaged offenders, when an angry victim comes face-to-face with the genuine remorse and vulnerability of the offender in a restorative justice meeting, the victim is challenged to re-examine his views and attitude toward the criminal. A realistic understanding of the offender and what lead him to offend are vital components in the victim's recovery and ability to experience closure over the victimisation.

These explanations can be plausibly generalised to include all criminal justice interventions. Restoration, closure, emotional conciliation, and healing will be promoted by an intervention more or less in proportion to the extent to which it proves successful in reversing mechanisms of moral disengagement on both sides of the criminal justice conflict. The onus, of course, is on the relevant criminal justice professionals, especially judges and facilitators, to detect the presence of mechanisms of moral disengagement and to use appropriate techniques for reversing them.[4]

---

4   On a note of caution, it would be counter-productive for professionals, and for anyone else, to suggest to victims, for example, that forgiveness is in any way expected of them. Whether victims reach that point during the intervention is entirely up to them. Although convenors of victim-offender meetings should aim to create the right conditions for emotional conciliation and healing, any expressions of remorse from offenders, or expressions of forgiveness from victims must be allowed to come naturally from them. Attempts by professionals to engineer reconciliation are likely to be recognised by the stakeholders as manipulation.

Social and moral development

Morality may be viewed as a socially constructed reality within which people's behaviour is judged in terms of right and wrong. Socially acceptable or obligatory ways of relating and behaving towards others are deemed right, while unacceptable behaviour is deemed wrong. Thus understood, morality plays an important function in society by facilitating social harmony and peaceful coexistence. Peaceful coexistence and social harmony are heavily dependent on the *moralisation* (moral enculturation) of society's individual members.

Individuals who are failed by the moralising process, and consequently fail to give effect to important values and social norms in their lives, become sources of danger and misery to others, as well as themselves as they face society's disapproval. Learning from one's own and other people's mistakes and misdeeds forms an important part of an individual's social and moral development.

There are good reasons to suppose that restorative justice meetings between offenders and victims are particularly effective in aiding the moral development of the participants. In a well run meeting there is an in-depth exploration of the details of the incident, its causes, and the many ways in which people were affected by it, including the offender. Even more importantly, participants voice their views about *why* this kind of behaviour is unacceptable and *why* it will not be tolerated. Finally, the meeting turns its attention to repairing the harm and the damage caused by the wrongful behaviour. Upon having responded in appropriate ways to repair the harm, the offender is welcomed back into the moral fold with a clearly articulated expectation that they will have learned from the incident and that they will do better in the future.

A restorative justice meeting offers a complete factual and moral picture of the wrongful behaviour, its circumstances, its causes, and its consequences. It also offers reasons as to *why* it is regarded to be wrong and unacceptable, and it demonstrates through example the need to put things right. It is hard to imagine a more powerful way of learning from mistakes and moral misbehaviour. As John MacDonald put the matter with respect to the moral development of young offenders:

> No one will argue against the right to silence, the right to legal representation, and competent counsel. But what we also suggest, and which lawyers can't offer, and don't want to offer, is the opportunity for the young offender to be educated from this experience. Young offenders have the right to learn the consequences of their crime. They have the right to understand how many other people it affects. They have the right to develop as full human

beings through this process. Now if you let the opportunity slip by, by handing it over to lawyers, you deny them all those developmental rights.[5]

In talking about learning from mistakes and moral development, we cannot ignore the hard cases: the relatively small number of recidivist offenders who commit a disproportionate amount of crime. Nothing so far seems to have helped in turning them around, and the question is whether restorative justice processes can make a difference where everything else has failed?[6]

When done right, restorative justice meetings can make a positive difference (with the possible exception of sociopathic and otherwise damaged individuals). If nothing else, a well organised and facilitated meeting can be a catalyst for the individual and their community to look for lasting solutions to underlying problems, and it is hard to think of a better way of breaking through to recidivist offenders and inducing in them a process of moral change.

Von Willigenburg has suggested that it is possible to influence for the better even the moral development of confirmed serious criminals – people who show in their behaviour over a long period "a propensity to commit seriously criminal acts, with an emphasis on predatory acts which are condemned in nearly all societies in all historical periods, like serious battery, rape, murder, theft and robbery."[7] The moral outlook of some of these criminals, according to von Willigenburg, may be morally deficient as a consequence of a limited range of morally formative experiences. If so, the remedy is to provide them with such experiences. This, it seems to me, is what well run restorative justice meetings provide.

The development of *moral maturity* in terms of character, moral awareness, sensitivity and perception, and good moral judgment is a gradual and complex process. Morally formative experiences are a crucial part of it. For example, the moral outlook and character of an eight-year-old will be influenced for the better if his parent hands in the lost wallet they had found with an amount of cash in it, and it will be influenced for the worse if the parent keeps the cash, throws the wallet

---

5   John MacDonald in "An Introduction to Family Group Conferencing", video by Real Justice.

6   There seem to be exceptions, especially comprehensive programs for recidivist youth which take young people out of environments where destructive influences are too powerful for them, and even for their families, to overcome. Giving young people the opportunity to absorb themselves in interesting and meaningful work and other developmental activities is what seems to be needed. Such programs, it would appear, are too expensive to be introduced on a wide scale and typically are of relatively short duration.

7   von Willigenburg 1996, p 127.

in a rubbish bin and says, "It's okay, son. Everybody does it." Through such episodes and experiences our moral views and characters are gradually formed, and it should not be difficult to see that restorative justice conferences expose offenders to morally formative experiences of the most powerful sort. In fact, von Willigenburg's own example describes an important part of what typically happens in a restorative justice meeting.

> Bringing criminals face to face with the consequences of their acts (for instance, by exposing them to their victims so that [they] may be in touch with the havoc caused in the lives of others) may induce a fine-tuning of moral perception. It may shape their imagination which is necessary for them to grasp what is real and to break through their self-preoccupied veil which partially seems to conceal from them what is going on when people are the victims of seriously criminal acts.[8]

Von Willigenburg also considers that seasoned criminals may not be moved as easily by new experiences because their moral outlook is resistant to change.[9] These are the unreachable criminals, as opposed to the merely unaware ones who are much more susceptible to morally formative experiences. The question then is whether the unreachable criminals are beyond all hope of changing their moral outlook. Is there anything that may radically influence their moral development? It seems that there is.

> What is needed here may be a kind of converting experience. This is the type of experience that forcefully invades into one's set of motivating reasons, because it is in some sense existentially moving. It is as if by shock one comes to see things one has never seen, one grasps the importance of reasons which one has never grasped.[10]

Recent research from the Netherlands mentioned by von Willigenburg seems to support the above hypothesis. Traumatic life events like the serious illness or death of a parent or beloved relative, or oneself becoming a victim of a serious offence, "sometimes have a surprising influence on the outlook of juvenile criminals ... [which] cannot be completely explained in terms of growing attachment, commitment and involvement."[11]

Von Willigenburg suspects that it is the unexpected nature of the life event which is crucial for bringing about a lasting and radical shift in outlook in these more difficult cases. However, the sense of moral crisis created by the relevant life event is a more plausible reason for

---

8   von Willigenburg 1996, p 137.
9   von Willigenburg 1996, p 138.
10   von Willigenburg 1996, p 138.
11   von Willigenburg 1996, p 139.

change in the offender instead, and the intentional induction of moral crises in a controlled and humane manner in the lives of otherwise unreachable criminals may well hold the key to combating recidivism.

There is no better way to induce and guide the outcome of such crises than in a restorative justice meeting, such as a conference or a sentencing circle where important people in the life of the offender are active participants. When, in addition to the victim and their supporters, the most important people in the offender's life confront the offender about the unacceptable behaviour and make it clear that they are shocked, hurt and ashamed by it, and that it is intolerable, there is tremendous pressure on the offender to re-examine their moral outlook and the kind of person they want to be.

In effect, restorative justice meetings confront recidivist offenders with a most critical choice. They can either choose to persist in their predatory ways and endure the pain of disapproval from their loved ones, or they can take a good hard look at the current course of their lives and ask themselves whether it really is worth it, considering all the pain and hardship it causes for everybody, not least of all themselves. This is a confronting life decision that a recidivist offender is pressed to make, but the key to its success lies in that the decision is socially forced on the offender by his own loved ones in a supportive and caring environment.

Such scenarios will see the majority of recidivist offenders choosing what is right over what is wrong – because choosing otherwise would be to choose rejection, isolation, and alienation from loved ones over being accepted by them and continuing belonging to them.

3. Emotional healing

Retzinger and Scheff have observed that there are two processes occurring side by side in a restorative justice conference – *material* and *symbolic* reparation. The process of material reparation results in a final settlement between offender and victim and typically consists of specific agreements about compensating the victim, community service etc. The process of symbolic reparation is less visible. It is composed of gestures and expressions of courtesy, respect, remorse, and forgiveness. According to Retzinger and Scheff, the core sequence, consisting of the offender's apology and the victim's forgiveness, is the key to reconciliation, victim satisfaction, and decreasing recidivism.

> It is the occurrence of the core sequence that generates repair and restoration of the bond between victim and offender ... Without the core sequence, the path towards settlement is strewn with impediments; whatever settlement is

reached does not decrease the tension level in the room, and leaves the participants with a feeling of arbitrariness and dissatisfaction. Thus, it is crucially important to give symbolic reparation at least parity with material settlement. Unless this is done, conferences may turn out, in the long run, to be only marginally better than traditional court practices. Symbolic reparation is the vital element that differentiates conferences from all other forms of crime control.[12]

These observations are able to be generalised beyond conferencing to restorative justice meetings in general. According to restorative justice philosophy, closure and emotional healing for the key participants are the vital characteristics of restorative outcomes, and symbolic reparation plays a recognisably important role in their achievement. Symbolic reparation is what allows and precipitates emotionally healing journeys being successfully undertaken by the relevant participants, a journey in the course of which people can rid themselves of the moral psychological and emotional burdens from an oppressive and hurtful past.

Such a journey is not the same for everybody. For an offender it may mean moving from a state of intense anxiety and fear, or from self-protective defiance and indifference, or from paralysing feelings of shame, humiliation, and worthlessness to a state of genuine remorse, empathy for the victim, being ready to make amends and repair the damage caused, and a feeling of inner confidence and resolve that they can, and will, do better in the future. For a victim the healing emotional journey may consist in moving from a state of insecurity and fear, or feelings of humiliation and shame, or from (justified) indignation, resentment and anger, or even from intense feelings of hate, to a state of acceptance of what happened, and even feelings of empathy for the plight of the offender and a readiness to forgive, or, at any rate, to put the matter behind them. Victim and offender supporters can also experience such emotional transition as part of their healing process, especially where they were seriously affected by the criminal incident.

Notwithstanding the differences, the healing processes of victims and offenders tend to be interdependent. For example, it is much easier for the victim to experience and extend forgiveness towards an offender who is genuinely apologetic and remorseful, as opposed to one who is disengaged and defiant. Similarly, it is much easier for an offender to drop their defensiveness in an atmosphere of respect, as opposed to one where they feel bullied and lectured by others with more power. Disrespectful treatment is likely to incite feelings of indignation and defiance even in an otherwise remorseful offender.

---

12   Retzinger and Scheff 1996, pp 316, 317.

These considerations highlight not only the importance of strong supporter representation in restorative justice meetings, but also the importance of good training for facilitators. Successfully navigating participants through their emotional journeys requires great skill. Emotions can run high in restorative justice meetings and they are a minefield for the unskilled and the unwary. Victimisation and re-victimisation are ever-present dangers in such emotionally charged situations and yet it is impossible to achieve a sense of closure, restoration and healing without dealing with the powerful emotions people experience in response to wrongful treatment and criminal violations.

4. Reintegrative shaming

According to John Braithwaite:

> Crime is best controlled when members of the community are the primary controllers through active participation in shaming offenders, and, having shamed them, through concerted participation in ways of reintegrating the offender back into the community of law abiding citizens. Low crime societies are societies where ... communities prefer to handle their own crime problems rather than hand them over to professionals.[13]

> The best place to see reintegrative shaming at work is in loving families ... Family life teaches us that shaming and punishment are possible while maintaining bonds of respect ... [F]amilies are the most effective agents of social control in most societies partly because of this characteristic.[14]

Properly understood, reintegrative shaming is present in what are generally accepted (by both participants and observers) to be highly successful restorative justice meetings. This is especially the case where important people in the offender's life are present as active participants in the meeting, such as in conferences and sentencing circles. Braithwaite's theory explains what is confirmed in conferencing practice (not less so than in sentencing circles) time and time again: the importance of involving as many significant members of the offender's family and friends, their community of support and care. When important and respected people in the offender's life disapprove of the offender's *behaviour* while at the same time show clear signs of respect and acceptance towards the offender *as a person,* positive impact on the offender is maximal.

It is under such conditions that it becomes most likely that the offenders themselves will internalise the distinction between *what they*

---

13   Braithwaite 1989, p 8.
14   Braithwaite 1989, p 56.

did and *who they are*. And, once this happens, they are almost certain to align themselves once again with their family and community and will not hesitate in rejecting their own wrongful behaviour as clearly unacceptable, which is, perhaps, the most critical first step in the process of successful restoration and healing – not only for them, but also for the victim. There are few things as distressing or aggravating to other participants, not least of all victims, as the defiance or indifference of the offender.

Having said that, there are a couple of points that must be clarified about the theory of reintegrative shaming. First, the theory provides only a partial explanation of what happens in restorative justice meetings. While it points unmistakably in the right direction with regard to the restoration and social reintegration of offenders, it does not go far enough to explain victim restoration and healing, which are just as important and are just as much part of restorative justice.[15]

The second point is that an unfortunate confusion surrounds the idea of reintegrative shaming. The confusion seems to be created by the word 'shaming,' as it is often taken to mean that offenders are shamed and humiliated in forums such as conferences. This is a misconception. For one thing, Braithwaite makes a clear distinction between *disintegrative* or *stigmatising shaming* on the one hand, and *reintegrative shaming* on the other.[16] Disintegrative shaming happens when *the person* is stigmatised, demeaned, and humiliated for what they did. Reintegrative shaming happens when the person's *behaviour* is condemned but their self-esteem and confidence are upheld through positive comments about them and gestures of forgiveness and (re-)acceptance.

Moreover, restorative justice experience shows that, with rare exceptions, a feeling of deep shame is evoked naturally and automatically in an offender as they are confronted with the harmful consequences of their actions. This confrontation with harmful consequences is most powerful when the offender hears directly from the victim, from the victim's supporters, as well as from their own supporters about the trauma, the tremendous emotional and/or physical harm they all suffered as a consequence of the offence. The intense feelings of shame and remorse thus generated are further compounded by the explicit disapproval of the offender's behaviour by their own supporters, especially their close family and friends. All this happens quite naturally in the course of discussions of what happened and how people have been affected and the way they see the behaviour.

---

15   To be fair, Braithwaite's theory is offender-focused by design. It does not purport to deal with victim justice issues and it is hard to see how it could.

16   Braithwaite 1989, p 55.

Therefore, there is no need to try shaming the offender intentionally, and people tend naturally and instinctively to avoid doing so in face-to-face meetings. Indeed, deliberate and intentional shaming and humiliation would be counterproductive, as it would be likely to either crush all self-confidence in the offender, or incite their indignation and defiance, having been left with no option but to reject their rejecters.

According to Braithwaite's theory, this must be avoided. To prevent it from happening, the often overwhelming experience of shame by the offender in a restorative justice meeting must be eased through reassuring and positive comments about the offender's person by the participants. This crucial role is played by the offender's supporters in the meeting. Of course, sometimes even the most supportive families may fail to show adequate support in emotionally charged situations, which can be overwhelming. In such situations a skilled convenor or facilitator can still ensure (through appropriate prompts) that the requisite support for the offender is forthcoming. For example, when Dad says that he was deeply shocked when he heard that Johnny vandalised the local bus shelter, or that he violently attacked someone at school, the facilitator should not miss the chance to ask "Why?" As with many things in a well-prepared and well-run meeting, the answer is predictable: "Because he is usually a good and responsible kid". The respect and acceptance expressed through such comments are vital to the offender's successful social reintegration.

Conclusions

Sketchy as they are, these explanations and theories are suggestive of the following hypothesis. In terms of providing long-term solutions to criminal behaviour, the success or failure of a criminal justice intervention, whether conventional or restorative, depends significantly on the degree to which it allows, or promotes, the realisation of the critical factors identified in these theoretical accounts. An intervention will tend to be successful to the degree that it succeeds in:

a) challenging the offender's (and victim's) psychological mechanisms of moral disengagement;

b) aiding the moral and social development of the offender, so that they learn from the experience;

c) aiding emotional healing from the trauma of the criminal incident; and

d) tempering unequivocal disapproval of the offender's wrongful *behaviour* (shaming) with expressions of respect for the individual as part of a community (reintegration).

Conversely, an intervention will fail to make a positive difference, and even tend to make things worse, to the degree that it fails to realise these factors.

Most importantly, these factors will tend to be realised by criminal justice interventions under conditions of empowerment and conversely, they will be difficult to realise under conditions of disempowerment (of the primary stakeholders involved).[17] This is an important sense in which the concept of empowerment is fundamental in restorative justice and the theory it gives rise to is overarching. It is the only plausible theory to provide a common thread for incorporating the various disparate theoretical explanations currently on offer into a unified, comprehensive account of restorative justice.

---

17 Generally, traditional criminal justice responses are more disempowering to the primary stakeholders than are restorative justice processes, and empirical data clearly confirms that the identified factors tend to figure prominently in restorative justice meetings, and hardly at all in court. (Sherman et al, 1998) But there can be equally significant differences between various restorative justice programs in terms of empowerment. Some are very good at it, and some are downright disastrous, with unacceptably low levels of stakeholder satisfaction and correspondingly high levels of victimisation, re-victimisation and recidivism. (Barton 1999b) Again, the degree to which the above critical factors are realised in these programs seems to be a direct function of this critical condition I refer to as the individual and collective empowerment of the primary stakeholders in the criminal justice response.

PART II

Implementing the Empowerment Model

4

A COMPARISON OF DIFFERENT RESTORATIVE JUSTICE CONFERENCING MODELS

In the previous chapter, various theories were presented as to what takes place in good restorative justice conferences. The question now becomes: how should such conferences be created and implemented? Not all facilitation models work equally well. Facilitation models vary between programs, and even between individual practitioners. The differences are mostly in terms of who gets invited, the order in which participants are asked to speak, and the kind of input participants are asked to contribute when they speak. This chapter explores the relative advantages offered by three facilitation models used around the world. These are, the facilitation model used in New Zealand Family Group Conferences; O'Connell's facilitation model, which is used in Community Accountability Conferences; and the new Empowerment model of this book, which builds on the strengths of the other models while also taking advantage of sound techniques and elements of mediation theory and practice.

General features of the three conference facilitation models

Following pre-conference preparations, the conference participants are seated in a circle, with no physical barriers between them. An impartial facilitator asks each participant one-by-one to tell their story and reflect on what happened, say how they were personally affected, and generally share their views and perspectives on the matter. Beyond this general description, there are significant differences in the processes that make up the various facilitation models. There are three identifiable stages in a well-constructed conferencing process. For ease of comparison the individual steps in all three facilitation models have been placed into one or the other of these main stages. These are *Exploration, Transition, and Agreement.* The restorative potential of each model will depend significantly on the extent to which it develops and makes use of each of these stages in practice.[1]

1. The First New Zealand Facilitation Model ('New Zealand model')

Modern day conferencing started with this facilitation model with the introduction of the *New Zealand Children, Young Persons and Their Families Act* 1989.

This facilitation model is still being used by Youth Justice coordinators. This first New Zealand model is clearly distinguishable from its variants, such as the facilitation processes used by the adult diversionary programs in that country, and the facilitation model used by South Australian Family Conferences for young offenders.

For example, many later models have eliminated the private session component, which is a dominant and important feature of the first New Zealand model. Private sessions will be discussed in more detail later. While there can be variations between regions and individual practitioners, the following is a description of the main features of the first New Zealand model.

Stage I: Exploration

1. Following preliminaries and introductions, the conference is formally opened and the police officer reads out the charges.

2. The offender is asked whether they admit or deny the charges. (The conference is unlikely to proceed further if the charges are denied. Instead, the case would be referred back to court.)

3. The victim is asked to tell what happened and express their views and feelings about the incident.

---

1   It needs to be kept in mind that practitioners of the various facilitation models may have different ways of marking the difference between steps and stages. For instance, among practitioners of the New Zealand Facilitation Model it is common to see categorisations in terms of
1. Information sharing;
2. Private family time; and
3. Presentation of the family's plan.

4. The offender is then asked to respond to the victim's account, and express their views on the matter.

5. Offender supporters and victim supporters (if present) are asked to comment and express their views on the matter.

6. Secondary stakeholders (professionals, such as police, social workers, advocates, etc) are given an opportunity to express their views on the matter and raise any concerns they may have.

Stage II: Transition

Absent in this model.

Stage III: Agreement

7. The offender and his or her family are given a private session to work out some kind of proposal to be presented to the victim and the police for their approval (as both have the right of veto).

8. When the family is ready, they present their plan to the conference.

9. The victim, and the police especially, are asked whether they accept the plan, or whether they want to see changes made to it. This usually results in constructive dialogue and fruitful negotiation between the key stakeholders.

10. All participants are given a chance to express their views on the proposed plan and/or the conference. However, final agreement or resolution is a matter between the victim, the offender, the police, and the coordinator – all of whom have the power to veto the agreement.

11. The conference is formally closed and participants are thanked for their contributions. Key participants may be contacted again in the days following the conference for their views, possible needs and suggestions for further action.

2. O'Connell's Facilitation Model ('O'Connell's model')

This model was developed and first used by Terry O'Connell in his capacity as a police officer in Wagga Wagga (1991, Australia), and was later adopted by the Australian Federal Police, and other police services in the United States of America, Canada, and the United Kingdom. It is also being used in many school communities and organisations in Australia, and is essentially the facilitation model that was taught by O'Connell's *Restorative Justice Group*.[2] Again, there are variants of O'Connell's model, as used and taught by training organisations, such as Transformative Justice Australia (TJA) and Real Justice. Variations are relatively small, but potentially significant.[3] The following steps in the process, including their order, are the most important in O'Connell's model.

Stage I: Exploration

1. Following preliminaries and introductions, the conference is formally opened and the offender is asked to tell what happened, and the way he or she became involved in committing the offence.

2. The offender is encouraged to reflect on the consequences that their actions have had on others and on themselves.

3. The victim is asked to tell what happened from their point of view, expressing their views and feelings about the incident, and explaining the way they were affected.

4. Victim supporters are asked to express their views on the incident, and explain how they were personally affected.

5. Offender supporters are asked what they thought and how they felt about the incident, providing insight into how they, and the offender, were affected by it.

6. Secondary stakeholders (professionals, such as police, social workers, advocates etc) are given an opportunity to express their views on the matter and raise any concerns they may have.

Stage II: Transition

7. The offender is given an opportunity to respond to the views and personal accounts of other participants.

---

2   This was a small but dedicated team in the Human Resources Command in the New South Wales Police Service, which has since been disbanded under immense political pressure from within and outside the service.

3   For example, the first edition of the Real Justice Training Manual left out O'Connell's Transition Stage. This appears to have been rectified in later editions.

Stage III: Agreement

8. The victim is given an opportunity to say what they wanted to see come out of the conference – the kind of outcome which would satisfy them.

9. The offender is given a chance to respond to suggestions made by the victim.

10. All participants are given a chance to express their views on what they thought would be a fair outcome. However, final agreement or resolution is a matter between the victim and the offender.

11. The conference is formally closed and participants are thanked for their contribution. Key participants are contacted again within a few days for their views, possible needs and suggestions for further action.

3. The Empowerment Model

Stage I: Exploration

1. Following preliminaries and introductions, the conference is formally opened and the offender and his or her supporters are asked if there was anything they wanted to say by way of starting the conference.

2. The offender is prompted to provide a detailed account of what happened, and the way her or she became involved in committing the offence.

3. The offender is encouraged to reflect on the consequences his or her actions have had on others, including the victim, their own family, friends, immediate community (school, neighbourhood, work place etc) and themselves.

4. The offender is asked outright whether there is any sense in which they believe that the incident was the victim's fault.

5. Offender supporters are asked for their views and feelings about the rightness and appropriateness, or otherwise, of what the offender has done, and what they think this means to the victim. They are also asked to say how they were personally affected by the incident.

6. The victim is asked to tell what happened from their point of view, expressing their views and feelings about the incident, and explaining the way they were affected.

7. Victim supporters are asked to express their own views about the incident, and explain how the victim and they personally were affected.

8. Secondary stakeholders (professionals, such as police, social workers, advocates etc) are given an opportunity to express their views on the matter and raise any concerns they may have.

9. All participants are asked to say briefly what they found to be most difficult about the incident.

Stage II: Transition

10. The offender is invited to respond to the views and accounts of other stakeholders, especially the victim and their close family and friends. Typically, offenders take this opportunity to express regret over what happened.

11. The victim and relevant others reply to the apologies, or silence, or whatever other response might have been given by the offender.

12. The principal offender supporters (such as the parents of a juvenile offender) address the victim and the principal victim supporters directly if they wish.

13. The victim and relevant others reply to the apologies, silence, or whatever other response might have been given by the principal offender supporters.

Stage III: Agreement

14. The offender and his or her supporters indicate if there was anything they have thought of doing to put things right with the victim.

15. The victim and his or her supporters indicate what *they* would like to see come out of the conference – the kind of outcome which they would consider to be fair. This is also an opportunity for them to respond to any proposals put forward by the offender and his or her principal supporters.

16. The offender is given a chance to respond to suggestions made by the victim and his or her supporters.

17. An opportunity is given for input from all other participants, both primary and secondary stakeholders, toward the agreement.

18. Time is allocated for a private session, or caucus. This may be skipped if so requested by the parties, but the opportunity is extended to all stakeholders in all circumstances. However, especially if the facilitator senses unease and tension in the room, or has concerns about the suggested agreement or can think of things that should be raised with either party, a confidential private session may be the most appropriate forum for it. In that case, they must indicate his or her intention to have a brief private session with *both* parties.

19. Upon reconvening, participants are given an opportunity to raise and discuss any further issues that may have come up during private discussions.

20. A final opportunity is given for all participants to express their views on the fairness, or otherwise, of the proposed agreement or outcome. However, final agreement or resolution is a matter between the victim and the offender (and, where applicable, other stakeholders that have a right of vetoing the agreement).

21. The conference is formally closed and participants are thanked for their participation. Key participants are contacted again within a few days to check how they feel about their conferencing experience and whether they have any special needs or suggestions requiring further action.

The three models compared

The Empowerment Model extends the strengths and advantages offered by the other two facilitation models. The three main stages of conferencing are all fully developed in the Empowerment Model. This is especially true of the transition stage which, by comparison to the other models, deals in a comprehensive way with the need of all participants to find peace and closure by making peace with others. By giving central importance to the transition stage where free and genuine expressions of remorse and forgiveness can take place between all participants, the Empowerment Model is a powerful model for peace making and peace building. The sequence of steps within each stage of the empowerment model has been carefully considered for consistency, bearing in mind everything we know today about conferencing philosophy and practice. They are also consistent with principles of mediation and conflict resolution in general, as well as with the moral and social psychological principles that underlie successful interpersonal exchanges, especially in situations of disagreement and conflict.

The three main stages and the most important steps that make up the Empowerment Model are discussed in turn. (The Stage and Step numbers below correspond to those identified in the Empowerment Model above.)

Stage I: Exploration

Steps 1 and 2. Who should speak first?

There are many advantages to having the offender speak first, rather than giving first say to a professional, such as a police officer, or even to the victim. Starting the conference with a police officer reading out the charges encourages a legal, as opposed to a moral framing of the incident and is more likely to set the tone for a surface approach, rather than a deep approach. Having the police officer read out the charges also signifies that the state has not transferred its power to the primary stakeholders. Signalling that secondary stakeholders are major players and decision makers in the conference process itself has a significant disempowering influence on primary stakeholders, especially on the offender and his or her supporters. This can create problems, particularly where a young and timid offender is already overwhelmed by the whole event. A police officer's disapproval is intimidating to most people, and when it is followed by strong words from an angry victim, a young or timid person may feel so overwhelmed that he or she may not be able to find his or her voice, let alone participate in a constructive manner. This, in turn, can lead to further aggravation of the officer and the victim, who may misinterpret the offender's silence and withdrawal as obstinacy, lack of remorse, or disrespect.

Having the charges read out by a police officer has other risks as well. One danger is that offenders may realise from the outset just how little the police know about the incident and may decide not to reveal all the relevant information about their involvement, giving only a scant account. In such cases, the offender will continue to hide behind the barrier of their concealment and neither the victim nor the offenders' own families will gain the necessary insight into the real causes of the problems that led to the wrongdoing in the first place. Another danger is that the police may not have all the smaller details of the offence correct, which provides an excuse for an angry and unrepentant offender to lash out at the police for "lying", instead of owning up to the wrongness of their own behaviour. An angry encounter with a police officer at the beginning of the conference can make it difficult to put things back on track, and the chances of this happening is much higher when it is the police who start the meeting with their version of events, which is all too often inaccurate and incomplete. Practitioners of the New Zealand model could eliminate a lot of tension and unnecessary aggravation from their FGCs by changing this aspect of their process – a fact which many coordinators realise, but feel powerless to change because of the fear that the police will not be happy about it.

Similar problems can be created by having the victim speak before the offender. In many cases the offender is already sorry for his or her victimising behaviour, and is mortified by having to face the victims in the presence of his or her own family and loved ones, whom they feel they have let down through what they did. A victim may not realise any of this, however, and may be assuming that the offender has no respect for them, and that they are not sorry for what they did. Consequently, they are in danger of pitching their contributions at a much higher level of angry disapproval than is appropriate, given the current state of mind and attitude of the offender. This in turn runs the danger of the offender feeling either crushed, or unnecessarily attacked by the victim, resulting in further withdrawal or a desperate and angry lashing out the victim and at others.

The above problems are best avoided by having the offender speak first. It is much easier for them to find their voice, and it is only fair that they get the first chance of owning and condemning their own behaviour, if that is how they have come to feel about it. Having them speak first encourages a fuller account of what happened, why or how certain things were done, or the way they went wrong. All of this gives other conference participants an accurate, up-to-date understanding of how the offender has come to see his or her behaviour after the event, and it helps them to pitch their own contributions accordingly. When an otherwise angry victim sees the remorse and genuine distress of the offender on account of what they have done, their anger and tension levels will tend to stabilise at the appropriate level and their contributions will be more likely to be constructive from the start. The same holds true for police officers and other participants. In short, having the offender speak first tends to give a smoother start for everybody involved.

Of course, if in spite of everything the offender refuses to own his or her behaviour, tries to make excuses, or if they are outright defiant and show a clear lack of caring about the consequences their actions have had on others, the victim and other participants are likely to respond with strong disapproval and the conferencing process quite appropriately takes on a different tone. While this is both natural and manageable, with good preparation and facilitation it rarely happens.

Strategies of dealing constructively with such situations will be discussed in more detail further below.

Step 3. Exploration of consequences

It is important to specifically explore the ways in which people have been affected by the wrongful behaviour in question. This will acknowledge and validate the hurt people have experienced and will show the rest of the participants the extent to which the offender is aware of the consequences their actions have had on others. This is especially important for the victim to hear and know, and also others such as the police. This element tends to be overlooked by the New Zealand model, but is given priority by both O'Connell's model and the Empowerment Model.

Step 4. Clarification of responsibility

Asking the offender outright whether, in their view, the incident is the victim's fault is a special feature of the empowerment model, and is designed to clear up any ambiguities the victim and other participants might have about the proper ownership of the wrongful behaviour in question by the offender.

Step 5. Who should speak immediately following the offender?

Giving the offender's supporters a say after the offender is a special feature of the empowerment model. O'Connell's model, which gives the offender first say, recommends a direct move from the offender to the victim. While this may be fine in a lot of cases, it is not the best option, and in some cases it can lead to disaster. It is always preferable to give the victim and other participants a thorough picture of the wrongful behaviour and its context before asking them to speak. Hearing the offender supporters' views and feelings about the whole incident is an important part of gaining such an all-round understanding of the offence, and it affords the victim time to grow comfortable with the process before being asked to speak.

This step is especially important if the offender is uncommunicative, or is showing defiance rather than remorse, or if they show any kind of reluctance to take responsibility for their harmful behaviour, such as when they make excuses or trivialise the offence they have committed. The reaction to such attitudes from victims tends to be dismay and anger, and it is best to have the offender's supporters express disapproval of the offender's behaviour before the victim, or any other participant, has their say. For example, if the offender is silent and uncooperative because they feel too intimidated, or over-whelmed by the whole event, then the supporter's explanation and interpretation of the offender's withdrawal will be met with under-standing, rather than with anger from the victim or a police officer who might misinterpret their silence as belligerence or disrespect.

The same principles hold in cases where the offender shows clear signs of defiance or if they try to trivialise matters. It will save all participants a lot of aggravation if the offender's defiance or inappro-priate attitude is first challenged by those closest to them, rather than by the victim or the police officer, or worse, the facilitator. If the people who are respected by the offender disapprove of such defiance and attitudes, as well as of the initial wrongdoing, then the need to see the offender own his or her behaviour unconditionally and showing remorse will no longer be so important to the victim. The victim gets the necessary validation from the important people in the offender's life, and this alone will be enough to save them from feeling re-victimised in the conference through the belligerence of the offender. This, once again, highlights the importance of inviting the right partici-pants and preparing them properly on both sides from the outset.

Step 6. Victims should also have their say ahead of secondary stakeholders

This choice reinforces the status of the victim as one of the key persons and decision makers in the conference. Having the victim speak before professionals are given the floor reinforces the initial framing of the problem or the offence in moral, rather than in legal terms, thus encouraging an exploration and resolution of the case in line with the deep approach, as opposed to the surface approach. This is something that has not been taken into account in the New Zealand model, but is clearly recognised by O'Connell's model and the Empowerment Model.

Step 7. Victim supporters

Having as many victim supporters present as offender supporters is important, and their contributions straight after the victim will serve to validate the victim's perspective, enhancing the victim's sense of empowerment. This safeguards the victim from feeling unduly vul-nerable and is essential in cases where the offender refuses to own his or her behaviour or is otherwise defiant, or even aggressive, towards the victim. In the absence of victim supporters the danger of re-victimisation is increased. Another important reason for bringing in a strong group of victim supporters is that they may all move on together in the conference, emotionally and cognitively, thus minimising the chances of the victim being told later by his or her close family and friends that they were too soft or did not stand up for themselves in the conference. The importance of strong victim support groups in conferences tends to be underestimated in the New Zealand model but is clearly recognised by both O'Connell's model and the Empowerment Model.

Step 8. Secondary stakeholder contributions

Following contributions from the primary stakeholders, professionals and other third party representatives should be asked for their thoughts and contributions. Giving voice to their perspectives any earlier than this runs the danger of stifling primary stakeholders with the institutional power that the representatives of the state bring with them.

Step 9. Review and refocus

Allowing participants to review and refocus on what is the most important to them about the incident is a unique feature of the Empowerment Model. This step is like a summary of the most important points raised in the exploration stage, and is especially important if contributions from secondary stakeholders have steered the discussion too much into a surface approach and legalistic technicalities. By briefly revisiting the moral and emotional dimensions of the offence, the conference will automatically refocus on the deep approach.

Stage II: Transition

Steps 10 to 13. Facilitating symbolic reparation and closure

The transition stage is absent in the New Zealand model. It is partly present in O'Connell's model and is a well developed feature of the Empowerment Model. This stage is extremely important, as this is where symbolic reparation, emotional conciliation and healing and peace making are quite deliberately given room to take place. This is the time that the facilitator devotes to the exchanging of positive conciliatory comments, the offering and acceptance of apologies and expressions of forgiveness. The mutual trust and good will generated becomes the ground for further conciliation and resolution in the remaining, agreement stage of the process.

It is a mistake to think that this stage in the process is too contrived, or that apologies and expressions of forgiveness must be totally spontaneous to be worth having. With possible but rare exceptions, when people do not feel like giving or accepting apologies, they simply don't. It is also important to appreciate that offenders and their supporters typically want to apologise if given a chance, but the intensity of the conferencing experience may be so overwhelming or preoccupying that they will miss the opportunity to do so, unless they are explicitly given the space. The same is true of the acceptance of apologies by victims and relevant supporters. Naturally, it would be clumsy and inappropriate for a facilitator to ask the offender or anybody else whether they would like to apologise, or show their forgiveness. The approach must be skilful and subtle, such as in the form of a simple question whether, say, the offender would like to say anything to the victim at this point, before moving on to working out an agreement. The relevant details and prompts for this are found in the Appendices.

Stage III: Agreement

Step 14. Putting things right

The resolution, or agreement stage should always start with the offender being given a chance to express any thoughts they might have had on how to put things right with the victim. If the offender has nothing prepared, nothing is lost by having asked them. However, where there has been prior family discussion about putting things right, it is important to allow such good will to show through to the victim and other participants, as it becomes an important component of strengthening the sense of emotional conciliation between the parties and helps to re-establish trust between them. Opening the resolution stage this way also allows the offender to be pro-active, to take the initiative, rather than being only reactive. This will serve to reinforce their sense of putting things right voluntarily because it is the right thing to do, instead of feeling forced to do something because they were asked. Similar reasons apply to giving the offender's supporters the same opportunity straight after the offender to indicate their thoughts on the important question of putting things right with the victim.

In these respects the empowerment model is, once again, more similar to the New Zealand model than to O'Connell's model. O'Connell's model recommends that the resolution stage start with the victim, which is fine, but not ideal. At the same time, while the New Zealand model allows the offender's family to create a proposal to be presented to the victim and other stakeholders, such a plan is worked out in response to being asked to do so. Thus, the good will and the prior thought that the offender and his or her family might have put into a plan before the conference may not have the chance to be clearly and spontaneously expressed. While this is no major handicap, it does signify a lost opportunity for reinforcing trust and furthering the cause of symbolic reparation, emotional conciliation, and healing.

Step 15. Victim empowerment and victim justice

The next step should be to ask, first the victim, and then his or her supporters, to say what *they* want to see come out of the conference, to indicate clearly their expectations in terms of an outcome that they would consider to be fair and satisfactory. This is also an opportunity for them to respond to any proposals put forward by the offender and his or her principal supporters.

Step 16. Offender empowerment

Following this, the offender, and then his or her supporters, should be given a chance to respond to the suggestions made by the victim and victim supporters. Unless the offender and his or her supporters are given the chance to speak their minds abut the proposals, they may feel pressured into an agreement that is not appropriate and they are not happy with. This should be avoided as much as possible.

Step 17. Input from the community

There should be an opportunity for input from all other participants, both primary and secondary stakeholders, towards the agreement. This will have the beneficial effect of making agreements realistic and meaningful for the offender and the victim as well as all concerned.

Step 18. Why private sessions are important

Following initial negotiations about outcomes and agreements, an opportunity for private sessions should be extended to all stakeholders. These sessions can take place individually or in a group, with or without the facilitator being present. In the event that the facilitator has special concerns that are best raised in private, they must indicate their intention to have a brief private session with *both* parties. These sessions allow for private discussions of sensitive issues that perhaps could not be raised in everyone's presence, and for double checking the viability of the proposed agreements. All matters discussed in private must remain confidential. It is up to the respective stakeholders to raise any points they want raised when the full conference resumes.

Private sessions are supposed to be an intrinsic feature of the New Zealand model, but they are completely absent, not only from O'Connell's model, but also it seems from all subsequent models, including relatively close variants of the New Zealand model. In many cases having a private session is unnecessary, although it can often be difficult to tell. Even the most experienced mediators are regularly surprised by what, against all appearances up to that point, can come out in private sessions. Therefore, in the Empowerment Model private sessions are optional, but strongly recommended. Private sessions are well tried and proven features of mediation practice, and conferences stand to benefit from them in similar ways. It is generally a good idea for the facilitator to be able to check in confidence with the participants how they are really feeling about the way the conference is going, what they really think about the proposed agreements, and whether the proposals are realistic and achievable. Also, many issues and special concerns that some participants may find impossible to raise in the full conference can be clarified and dealt with in a private session, and strategies may be found to raise those concerns in an appropriate way in negotiations when the conference reconvenes.

Step 19. Post-caucus negotiations

Before any agreements are finalised, there should be an opportunity for participants to raise any further issues that may have come up in private sessions. If need be, initial proposals must be modified through a democratic process of negotiation until everybody, or at least the principal stakeholders are happy with the agreement.

Step 20. Final checking

When it looks like a final agreement has been worked out, there should be a final opportunity for all participants to express their views on the fairness or otherwise of the proposed agreement. However, final agreement should be a matter between the victim and the offender, and only after that between other stakeholders who may sometimes have a right of veto to an official agreement being reached. In some programs this may include professionals and representatives of the state, such as the conference coordinator and the police.

5

FOR FACILITATORS: A GUIDE TO RUNNING CONFERENCES

Facilitating a conference can at times look like a daunting task, especially when you are starting out. In reality, it is relatively easy, provided that you have a clear idea about your role, learn the relevant skills of mediation and facilitation and are prepared to follow a few basic guidelines. Consistently good practice is neither automatic, nor dependent on luck. Rather, it is created at will by practitioners who know what they are doing. You can secure consistently good results by preparing well and using the approach to facilitation outlined in this book. Participant satisfaction will also depend on these factors, as well as on the quality of the follow-up work you provide. This chapter covers these three components of a conferencing intervention: preparation, facilitation and follow-up.

The most important guiding principle behind everything you do should be that of *empowerment*, namely, *the individual and collective empowerment of the primary stakeholders to deal with their matter the way it is right for them, in negotiation with one another.* All the suggestions and guidelines for good practice in this book are grounded in this principle. So, if at any point you are wondering why it is suggested that you do this or that, the only compelling answer should be that by conducting your facilitation that way, you will maximise the chances that the key stakeholders will be empowered to deal with their issues in a way that is right for them. If any particular suggestion in this book regarding good practice does not, in your view, meet this objective of empowerment, then you cannot, in good conscience, follow it. However, before you decide to depart from any of these suggestions, you should be very clear about your reasons for doing so, and make sure that your proposed departure will serve the empowerment of the primary stakeholders better. When such a situation arises, then the right thing for you is to follow your own judgment concerning the finer details, but never lose sight of the principle and main objective.

Indeed, it is important for the evolution of good restorative justice practice, as well as for your own development as a professional facilitator, that you experiment with new ideas and approaches, if they seem promising or compelling. However, this is best attempted after you have mastered the basic facilitation system provided in this book. The guidelines in this book have been formulated, not merely on the basis of restorative justice theory, but more importantly on the basis of first hand observation of many conferences by the author, as well as practical experience in interpersonal conflict resolution as a mediator and facilitator. The system presented here is firmly based on experience. Your mastery of it will mean that you and the people in your conferences will be safe even in the event that you experiment, because you will be able to return to the safety of this system whenever a meeting gets into trouble.

The conferencing process

Any conferencing intervention may be usefully thought to consist of three main parts, namely pre-conference preparations, the actual conference, and post-conference follow-up. The conference itself, as we saw earlier, is made up of a number of stages and steps through which conference participants are guided by the facilitator. Thus, the structure of the conferencing process is as follows:

Part I: Preparation
Part II: Facilitation
           Introduction and Preliminaries
           Stage I: Exploration
           Stage II: Transition
           Stage III: Agreement
           Closing
Part III: Follow-up

The strength of any conferencing system will depend on the quality of its individual components, just as a chain will be only as strong as its weakest link. For example, without proper preparation a conference may be compromised from the start, especially if strong support is not secured for the victim and the offender. Similarly, without good facilitation a conference can all too easily go wrong, especially when the parties disagree and emotions run high. Again, without proper follow-up, a lot of the progress achieved by participants in the actual meeting can be undone, such as when key stakeholders are not kept informed and when agreements are not honoured.

The facilitator must ensure that in the meeting itself all the important (material and emotional) issues are properly explored. You must also ensure that all key participants are given the opportunity for symbolic reparation. This should occur in the transition stage, before helping the parties work out a conference agreement. Finally, in facilitating negotiations towards a final agreement, the facilitator must ensure that the key parties are appropriately empowered to speak their minds and that nobody feels pushed around in what is meant to be a consensual and democratic decision making process. The remainder of this chapter will focus on the nuts and bolts of how you as a facilitator can make all of this happen, even in difficult cases. Please also make sure to read the step-by-step explanations of the various steps and stages in the process. These were covered in the previous chapter. This way you will be able to make a more informed decision if you are tempted to dismiss or leave out any part of the process, the prompts for which are all detailed in the Appendices.

Part I: Pre-Conference preparations

Good preparation lays the foundation for a successful conference. Pay particular attention to the following:

1. *Inviting participants, setting a suitable time, and organising an appropriate venue, refreshments, etc.*

The conferencing program within which you will be convening the conference is likely to have guidelines in place concerning such preparatory matters. You should work as closely as possible to such guidelines while having regard to the following points:

a) Even though some timid or reluctant invitees may need reassurance and even gentle persuasion, their participation must be voluntary. Nobody should be coerced or tricked into attending restorative justice meetings. Giving reluctant participants misleading information is not only wrong, but is likely to rebound on you: people's autonomy cannot be violated without undermining trust and the fundamental values and principles that underlie restorative justice outcomes.

b) Victim participation is very important, and therefore you should try to ensure that the victim is properly informed about the nature of the proposed meeting. Their attendance should not be jeopardised by factors such as an unsuitable time or inappropriate venue, which should be a neutral and safe environment for all participants.

c) Ensuring that the victim and offender are well supported is the best, and often the only way to ensure that the conference will be a constructive event. Strong support is especially important when there is a power imbalance between the parties, or when the key stakeholders appear timid or fearful, or when the offence is serious or people have been seriously affected. Creation of a strong community of participants will also be your insurance that people in your conference will not be victimised or re-victimised, and that the voices of reason will prevail over expressions of extreme views and emotions. Regardless of the done thing in your particular program (unfortunately, all too many programs neglect to pay sufficient regard to this point), creating strong communities of participants in the way explained here is the only way you will be able to do justice to the importance of what is being asked of you as a conference convenor.

d) The appointed time must be suitable for both parties, including the crucial supporters on both sides. The venue must be a neutral one, so that neither party feels uncomfortable about the environment. For example, it could be intimidating for either party if the meeting were to be held in the other side's home environment. These matters should always be checked with both sides and their wishes accommodated as much as possible. Should it be impossible to avoid all bias in terms of a venue, the imbalance can be compensated for by making sure that there is a robust support group at the meeting for the disadvantaged party.

e) Making refreshments available is good practice, though not essential. A meeting may go on for a long time, and having refreshments available will create a more relaxed atmosphere, which can become especially important in the more difficult cases where you may need to see each party separately in a private session, while giving the others a break. Also, having refreshments available at the end of the formal part of the meeting will encourage participants to stay for a while and engage in informal conversation, which will continue to reinforce the reconciliation process well beyond the conference.

2. Preparation of participants for the meeting

Essentially, this requires that intending participants be given full and accurate information about the proposed meeting. Such information should include the principal aim of the meeting and an outline of the facilitation process which will be used. Further, the provision of accurate information to invited participants about their rights, such as the right to refuse participation and/or the conditions under which the case may be sent to court, etc, is important for securing their informed participation. Intending participants must be aware, for example, not only of what they can realistically expect from the proposed meeting, but also whether dealing with the matter by way of conference, as opposed to court, will be likely to affect their future options, such as the victim's ability to claim state compensation for criminal injuries, and the offender's ability to have a defended hearing of the case, unbiased by any admissions made in the conference. If any such areas are unclear from a legal point of view, then intending participants should be alerted to them beforehand. They should also be encouraged to seek independent legal advice whenever such considerations are present, even though this runs the risk of some legal advisers being unduly negative or discouraging to their clients. The importance of informed consent, however, overrides such considerations. The decision is not yours to make, but your clients'.

Finally, briefing participants about the process is also important when legislation or established protocols have a potentially negative impact on the process. Many jurisdictions, such as those in New Zealand, for example, require that a conference start with the charges against the youth being read out by a police officer or a prosecutor and that the alleged offender accept the charges before the conference proceeds. As suggested earlier, a police officer starting the conference can be intimidating to people – and therefore not the best way to proceed. However, its negative influence can be minimised by taking care to explain to the offender and their family beforehand that this is a formal requirement that needs to be fulfilled before the conference can go ahead.

All such information is empowering and will allow intending participants to take part in an informed and confident manner, as they are able to prepare themselves better both mentally and emotionally. Chapters 6 to 10 are addressed to various categories of participants. You may wish to refer participants to the relevant chapters and sections applicable to them.

3. Preparing the facilitation instruments: seating plan, scripted prompts and crisis management plan

The importance of these for consistently good facilitation practice cannot be overemphasised. These instruments can be used for all conferences, but they must be customised for each case. All of these are included in the Appendices.

4. Preparing the conference venue

Allow sufficient time for organising the conference venue before the arrival of the participants. Arriving half an hour or so before the conference should be adequate to allow you to arrange the room for the meeting, organise refreshments and, ideally, prepare separate waiting areas for the two key parties. In particular, you should ensure that the seating is all set up beforehand. If you have a finalised seating plan you may choose to write the participants' names on separate pieces of paper, or onto stickers, and place these on the appropriate chairs. This will make seating of the participants less chaotic and more dignified, especially where large groups are expected.

Alternatively, you can show each person to their allocated seat, unless, of course, you decide to allow participants to sit wherever they wish. Whichever way you decide, it is a good idea always to have spare, blank seating plans with you, in case you have to make (a new) one up during introductions.

5. Reception of participants before the conference

The two main parties should be allowed to wait in different rooms, or different parts of the reception area. Sometimes a group of participants will choose to wait and chat outside the building, while the other party waits in the reception area. If there is no other way of ensuring a comfortable distance between the principal parties, it is a good idea to let the victim and their supporters into the conference room, while the other party waits outside until everything and everybody is ready for the start. Ideally, the conference room is already set up before the parties arrive. It is a good idea to make refreshments available during this time, especially if there is a delay in starting the conference.

6. Seating of the participants

It is often easiest if secondary stakeholders, such as social workers and police officers, are allowed into the conference room before the other parties, and are seated first. People who are not going to participate in the conference, such as observers, assistants, and security officers should be seated outside the circle, leaving a reasonable distance between them and the actual participants. Following this, it is a good idea to let the victim and their supporters be seated next, so that they can also be settled before the offender and their supporters are asked in to be seated.

Regardless of how you seat the various parties, it is important to make sure that you are ready to start as soon as everybody is seated. It causes unnecessary distress and awkwardness if the facilitator keeps the parties waiting after everybody has been seated. Still trying to get organised while everyone is sitting there waiting for you in painful silence, trying to avoid each others' eyes, makes you look unprofessional, and it can start undermining your credibility as a competent facilitator. To avoid such episodes, you must make sure to have your pen, seating plan and scripted prompts open and ready for an immediate start as soon as the last person in the circle has taken their seat.

Part II: Conference facilitation

A well-prepared and well-facilitated conference is not unlike the performance of a choir or orchestra. Just as the conductor is able to elicit and bring together the many different tunes and sounds from members of the orchestra at the right time and in the right order in the performance of a great symphony, the facilitator of a restorative justice conference can elicit and bring together, at the right time and in the most efficient order, the most constructive contributions from the various stakeholders. Doing so requires that you are methodical in applying the present guidelines.

Some facilitators like to explain the process in great detail, even waving at participants a copy of the legislation that forms the legal basis for the conference. This is unnecessary and is a distraction. It is best not to clutter participants' mental space with such details. They should be allowed to keep their minds on the content of the conference and its inter-personal, moral dimensions. As long as you know what you are doing, participants will be more than happy to leave the finer points of the process to you. If you do choose to explain the process in the conference, make it very brief and avoid talking about Laws and Acts of Parliament, which may inadvertently set the tone for a legalistic, surface approach. This was explained in Chapter 2.

As a facilitator, you need to be clear about what you are trying to achieve. Under no circumstances should you make restorative justice, or even emotional conciliation or material agreement between the parties, your direct objective. Doing so will make you more likely to deviate from remaining impartial throughout the process. Such goals are best kept at the back of your mind as valued outcomes, which, however, must be left to the stakeholders to realise. They are not your direct responsibility.

Your responsibility is *to create the best possible environment in which all stakeholders are empowered and can freely decide, in discussion and negotiation with one another, how to deal with their issues in the way that is right for them.* Whether they choose to deal with those issues "restoratively" or not is a matter for them to decide, not for you or any other secondary stakeholder. The proposed agreement of course must stay within the law and within the precepts of morality and social convention. Approaching your work with the above goal in mind will quickly earn you the trust and respect of both parties, which is critical for conferencing success. Using judgmental language, and even the language of restorative justice philosophy to encourage reconciliation between the parties is one of the worst things you can do, and will undermine your credibility with the parties.

As the facilitator it is useful to bear in mind that each step of the conferencing process has two main elements. These are:

1. *Prompts and other facilitation techniques.* As explained below, it is good practice to prepare in advance the most common prompts so that you can keep glancing at them during the conference. They will serve you both as a guide and as a checklist against which your progress through the process can be monitored. A facilitator's script is provided in Appendix 1, and prompts for a crisis management plan in Appendix 2.

2. *Participant contributions and the realisation of certain goals and sub-goals by the stakeholders in the meeting.* The conference gives participants the opportunity to resolve issues to their satisfaction. But such a resolution is unlikely to occur unless a shared understanding of what happened is achieved first. That is to say, arriving at such an understanding is a sub-goal that must be realised by all those present before an agreement can be reached. Participants need to know, for example, how the offender got involved in the incident, and the way people have been affected by it. The sharing of such information between participants should take place relatively early in the conference (exploration stage). The facilitator can help by using prompts, such as, "Please, tell us what happened? Then, what happened?" and "How has this affected you?"

By using the appropriate prompts and facilitation techniques, the facilitator enables participants to reach many similar sub-goals in the conference. Thus, in a manner of speaking, in a conference there are two interrelated "scripts" running in parallel, and it is the facilitator who must be mindful of both. Participants will be engrossed in the *content* of the conference, as they should be, and it is the facilitator's task to take care of the complex *process* just mentioned. Therefore, (2) is achieved by means of (1). The facilitator's prompts (1) consist of questions, gestures and suggestions that the facilitator uses to elicit relevant responses and contributions from participants (2).

Participants' responses and the achievement of particular goals and sub-goals in the conference can be covert or overt. For example, an important goal is for all participants to have their chance of saying how they were affected by the incident, and it is not difficult to tell whether this has been achieved or not. By comparison, a participant's degree of frustration or satisfaction with the way the conference is going can be more difficult to ascertain as can be their degree of moral and emotional engagement. Quite often these must be inferred by the facilitator from overt, if subtle, signs – such as the degree of tension or ease with which participants interact. While this may sound difficult in the abstract, it is not too difficult to be aware of in real life conferences. It also becomes increasingly easier through training and practice. If ever in doubt, you can ask the relevant participants outright: "How do you feel about the way this conference is going so far?" "Why do you feel that way and what would you like to see happen?" and then invite others to engage with the views expressed: "What do others think if that?" Also, brief private sessions may be a useful way to find out how things are going for particular people. Mediators use this technique as a matter of course, and there is no reason why conference facilitators should not make equally good use of it.

However, as already indicated, the aim should never be to manipulate any participant into thinking or feeling in a certain way. Manipulation is self-defeating, as it is likely to be picked up and resented by participants. The sole aim of the facilitator must be to provide the conditions under which participants can speak their minds so that all issues can be dealt with the way it is right for *them*. Everybody has the right to intellectual, moral, and emotional self-determination, and it would be inappropriate and patronising of a facilitator to expect, for example, expressions of forgiveness from a victim, or even remorse from an offender. As a facilitator, you are not in a position to expect a conciliatory spirit from any participant, but must ensure that you bring in appropriate support people who will provide the meeting with balance and reasonableness, as has been described in earlier chapters. Ultimately, individuals value their autonomy and are responsible for their own thoughts, actions, feelings, and healing. They will complete their respective moral and emotional journeys as, and when, they are ready. The aim of the conference should be to prepare the ground and maximise opportunities for people to at least commence such healing journeys, besides enabling the parties to find practical solutions and resolutions for the causes and the immediate consequences of the incident in question.

Having said that, there are some clearly identifiable responses that a facilitator should seek from participants at every step in the process. The facilitator should not move onto the next step before providing an opportunity for the appropriate responses to be elicited from the relevant participants. Thus, as already explained, one of the first objectives of a facilitator is to get the offender talking about the incident and allowing them a clear opportunity for *taking* responsibility for their wrongful behaviour. Such an opportunity should be given before the other participants, such as the victim or the police officer, inevitably start *holding* the offender responsible. In the event that an offender simply cannot find their voice, or remains disengaged, then their family and other close supporters should be encouraged to speak on behalf of the offender and express their own views on the matter in terms of what they think of the offence, and who they think is properly responsible for it, and indeed explain to the meeting why the offender seems unable to talk about matters at that point.

But, regardless of which way this is achieved, unless a clearly recognisable space is created at the beginning for the other party to acknowledge responsibility for what happened, an understandably upset victim, and/or an equally unimpressed police officer, are likely to start off on a less than favourable note. This can cause a great deal of unnecessary aggravation all round. Following a rough start of this kind, where anger and suspicion are aroused, a conference can be hard to recover, and such setbacks are best prevented. You should ensure by means of the appropriate prompts that the offender has an opportunity to take responsibility at the outset for the wrongful behaviour in question, or, in the event that the offender is reluctant, that an opportunity is given to the offender's supporters to acknowledge the offender's responsibility. One way or another, there must be an opportunity for acknowledgment that the victim is not to blame.

However, it is not the role of the facilitator to decide the offender's responsibility, let alone extort it from them. The facilitator's role is simply to allow an opportunity for responsibility to be acknowledged by the relevant party. In cases where this does not happen, they must enable the rest of the participants, especially the victim and their supporters, to have their say on the matter. It is a serious (and common) mistake to gloss over anyone's rationalising behaviour in an attempt to avoid a scene being created by an unimpressed victim. The victim's satisfaction and healing is undermined if he (or she) is not given the opportunity to say how he feels about the rationalising behaviour in question, and challenge it. This opportunity can easily be provided by prompting the victim: "Is there anything you would like to say in response to that?" For, if such matters are glossed over, instead of confronted, trust will never be established between the parties and true reconciliation becomes next to impossible.

Another crucial part of the conference is the transition stage. This is where emotional conciliation hopefully comes to the fore. The preceding exploration stage must be geared towards maximising the likelihood that sincere apologies will be offered and accepted in good faith. If the offender is openly defiant, it is a good idea to ask the offender's supporters about their views on what the offender just said or did. The intention here is not to change the offender's mind, or extort an apology from them, but allow them to hear what other people think of their attitude. It will give them something to think about, and it will shield the victim from feeling re-victimised.

Expressions of forgiveness and re-acceptance constitute a very important part of the healing process for both the victim and the offender, but also for their respective families and friends. Provided that everything was done well by the facilitator up to this point, it would be rare for the victim and relevant others not to accept sincerely offered apologies. Conferencing experience shows that the offender's supporters often have a need themselves to extend their apologies to the victim. Hence, it is good practice to provide an opportunity for them to do so, whether or not the offender apologises.

If, in the improbable case that the offender's supporters are also hostile towards the victim, their re-victimisation can and must be avoided by asking all the victim's supporters, as well as secondary stakeholders for their views on the other party's approach and position. The joint support of these people should be enough to give the victim the validation they need. This outside possibility of the other party turning on the victim in the conference also reinforces the importance of having strong victim support present. An experience of re-victimisation should be viewed as the worst possible outcome in a conference, and it deserves every effort to ensure that it does not happen.

Unfortunately, this consideration tends to be ignored or is all too readily compromised by facilitators and programs where restorative meetings are convened with an offender-focused, welfarist ideology. Partisan agendas, such as saving the young offender from court, a criminal conviction, and gaol, no matter how worthwhile, will compromise facilitator neutrality and credibility with the other party and must, therefore, be left to welfare workers and youth advocates who can be present. *Neutrality* (not having a stake in the outcome) and *impartiality* (not taking sides) are the twin pillars of facilitator credibility and must be regarded as inviolable principles by practitioners in restorative justice.

Preparing the facilitation instruments

The facilitation instruments consist of a seating plan, a structured facilitation plan made up of scripted prompts for facilitating the conference, and scripted crisis management plans. As indicated earlier, the importance of having these worked out in advance cannot be over-emphasised. A clear seating plan and well-prepared prompts will serve as guides and as checklists against which you can readily tell who is sitting where, and quickly assess where you are up to in the conference process, what has been accomplished, and what still remains to be done. Without these, even the most experienced facilitators will overlook important points that they otherwise fully intended to cover, remembering them only after the event. Such retrospective realisations, unfortunately, will do little for the people who were short-changed by the oversight. Distrust of scripted plans and prompts is widespread in some places. (A good example being New Zealand where an explicit anti-script culture has developed.) This is unfortunate and a sure prescription for sloppy, inconsistent practice – defence of which in the name of flexibility and spontaneity is as inane as it is misguided.

Checking your progress against a plan which you have carefully prepared before the conference will maximise your chances of delivering the best possible process every time. Co-facilitating a conference, whereby you share the work with another facilitator, is a good idea, as it provides you with more time and mental space to keep on top of what is happening, not to mention the backup support your co-facilitator can give you when you find yourself at a loss as to what to do next. Unlike in mediation, co-facilitation systems are not common in conferencing programs, which makes well-prepared conference plans even more important. But even with a co-facilitation system, having a jointly agreed upon plan holds all the advantages of knowing in advance where the process is headed and what comes next. A well-prepared conference plan allows facilitators to synchronise their respective roles, enhancing their ability to deliver a smooth, effective process. Let us now consider each facilitation instrument in more detail.

(a) Preparing the seating plan

Whenever possible, participants should be seated in a circle, without any barriers between them. In terms of seating positions, it is useful to develop some kind of system, a consistent way of seating participants, so as to obviate the need for memorising which party is sitting where in your conferences. A good example is seating the offender and their supporters always to your right, victims and their supporters always to

89

your left, and secondary stakeholders always opposite to you. See the Diagram in Appendix 1. If you feel that seating the offender and the victim directly opposite to each other would create undue discomfort, you should take this into account in deciding the exact seating, in consultation with the key participants. It is also a good idea to check beforehand with the key stakeholders, particularly the victim and the offender, whether they would prefer having particular supporters sitting next to them in the conference.

Alternatively, you may decide to let people sit wherever they feel most comfortable, and then fill in their respective names and roles on your seating plan during introductions. If you are inclined to favour this approach, keep in mind that those who enter the room early cannot make a very informed decision about where to sit, since they will not know where the other participants are going to seat themselves relative to them. Furthermore, those who enter the room towards the end will have little choice but to take whatever seats are left, regardless of how uncomfortable they might find sitting in that particular spot.

Sometimes new participants may turn up, and others who intended to be there may not be able to make it. Be prepared to alter your seating plan, or make up a new one.

If people have already been seated and you don't want to disturb them, or if you would like everyone to find their place as they feel comfortable, then while they are still chatting, go around informally and record each person's name on your seating plan, greeting them and introducing yourself to them as appropriate. Another option may be to write people's names on the plan as they introduce themselves to the group, in the early part of the conference. Doing so, however, can prove rushed and messy, especially if you miss someone's name, or their relationship to the principal parties. It is advisable, therefore, to have your plan pretty much completed before you open the conference and before formal introductions begin.

Regardless of how you arrive at a final seating plan, make sure that you always have one completed by the time the Exploration stage of the conference gets underway. A clear seating plan will act as your compass, so that you know exactly who is sitting where at all times. Using a seating plan, such as that shown in Appendix 1, write the names of the people inside circles, and write a couple of key words that will remind you of their respective roles or relationship to the key participants, against the circles on the periphery.

(b) Preparing the scripted prompts

A script, such as that given in Appendix 1, will act as a guide for what to do next at every point, and as a checklist for working your way through the conference. Without an appropriate script to check your progress against, it can be all too easy to miss covering each important issue at the appropriate time. Chances are, of course, that you will not have to verbalise every prompt on your list, as many of them become redundant when strong groups get down to the task and sort matters out. Even so, having a well-structured script before you enables you to know at all times exactly how far through the process the conference has progressed, and what remains still to be done. In reading through the scripted prompts given in Appendix 2, keep in mind that each one has been included for a reason.

Regardless of the type of facilitation process you decide to use, you can prepare the prompts you intend using in the meeting according to the conference structure described in Chapter 4. That structure is:

Introduction and Preliminaries
Stage I: Exploration
Stage II: Transition
Stage III: Agreement
Closing

In light of the preliminary information you obtain about the case at hand from the referral and from talking to the parties in the preparation stage, you can tailor your prompts in advance by filling in the spaces and making appropriate modifications to the scripted prompts provided in the Appendices. These prompts apply equally well to the three conferencing models that were compared and discussed in Chapter 4: the Empowerment Model, O'Connell's model, and the New Zealand model of conference facilitation.

While facilitating the conference, you should have these customised prompts before you, as well as the seating plan, reading from them and checking your progress against them, ticking them off one by one as you get through them. You should also have the crisis management plan tucked away ready for use, in case you need it. Finally, make notes of thoughts and questions that may occur to you as the conference proceeds. This way you will not forget to raise them with the relevant participants in the conference, or later in a private session, or indeed after the conference, as you deem appropriate.

It will be simplest and easiest, especially when you are just starting out, to read out the prompts as prepared beforehand. While this may feel awkward at first, it will save you from common problems, such as using judgmental language, rambling, and straying from the intended process. These are all too easily done if you are nervous or disoriented, and you can take it for granted that you are going to feel nervous and disoriented from time to time.

If you learn to use and rely on your scripts in the way just explained, nobody will even notice, and you can feel confident that you are not going to make a mess of any case entrusted to you, but will do the best that anybody can do to help your charges sort matters out for themselves in the way it is right for them. Eventually, the right phrases and lines will roll off your tongue with ease, at which stage your scripted prompts will act more as checklists against which you can monitor your direction and progress.

(c) Preparing appropriate crisis management plans

In addition to the standard, scripted prompts, prepare appropriate crisis management plans and have them ready for use in the conference, should a crisis situation arise. See Appendix 2 for a template for a crisis management plan. A crisis situation can arise, for example, when the offender and/or their supporters blame the victim for what happened, when a victim remains unmoved and unduly harsh, in spite of conciliatory overtures from the offender, or when offender supporters lecture and bully the offender, instead of being supportive. The last type of situation, for example, can result in a young person disengaging completely in self-defence, which will prevent them from responding properly to the victim's concerns, potentially creating a whole set of complications that can put the meeting in jeopardy.

Crisis management plans are designed to clarify the critical issues and facilitate their resolution, while protecting the relevant parties from being alienated, victimised, or revictimised in a highly charged, volatile situation. You should be able to get a good sense of the likelihood of these kinds of emergencies arising in the meeting from your initial contact with the various parties beforehand. Inviting strong support groups on both sides is one useful preventive measure but giving prior thought to what could still go wrong and working out promising ways of responding to crises is equally important. With such thorough preparation you will be unlikely to be caught off-guard. You will not be at a loss as to how to deal with crises, which, in spite of careful preparations, do crop up every now and then in restorative justice meetings.

In terms of a practical guide, study the crisis management plan provided in Appendix 2, and modify it as you see fit for each case. Have this at hand, and any other emergency scripts that you may develop, in case things start getting difficult in a conference. Preparation of scripted prompts for the crisis management plan requires the same kind of advanced planning as does the preparation of scripted prompts for the standard, smooth-flowing conference. If you find the scripts provided for either of these not quite appropriate, you should develop your own scripts by taking the relevant prompts and parts from the sample scripts provided. It will help the smooth flow of your process if you customise your prompts by filling in the appropriate names in the gaps provided in advance of the conference.

Such detailed preparation before every conference may seem tedious, but it is essential for consistently good conferencing practice. While conferences in general have a great deal in common, each one of them is still unique. Therefore, each one must be approached as a fresh case, with its own set of individual and interpersonal dynamics, and potential for success and failure. By preparing in advance your seating plan, and by individualising and contextualising the two sets of standardised prompts, you will attune yourself both to the conference issues and to the various personalities you will be dealing with in the meeting. Such prior consideration of the issues and of the invited participants will prepare you to anticipate possible difficulties and handle them with skill and confidence.

Part III: Post-conference

1. Follow-up contact with the key participants.

The key participants – victim, offender and their closest supporters – should be contacted within one to three days to check how they feel about the way things went. You should also check with them whether there is anything you can help them with. Some participants may need such contact to help them interpret or understand better some of the things that happened in the meeting. Such contact is also an opportunity for them to debrief, and a valuable opportunity for you to gain a more reliable sense of what has been achieved, what still needs to be done, and whether you should try out something different with similar problems or cases in the future. You can also take the opportunity to ask these participants for suggestions about the process, whether they would have preferred some things to have been handled differently. All such information can be valuable for your personal and professional development and the overall evolution of good practice in this relatively new area.

2. Monitoring fulfilment of agreements and keeping relevant stakeholders informed about progress

Having an active monitoring system in place is extremely important. All parties need to be kept informed about progress and difficulties concerning the conference agreement. Such a system encourages people to honour their promises under the agreement. From the offender's point of view, if nobody seems to care about how things are going, it is much easier for him not to do what he knows he ought to do. By contrast, if people show an interest in how things are coming along, that in itself provides a powerful incentive to complete the task, even if it has become onerous.

Why should we ensure that conference agreements are honoured? First, because, typically, a conference agreement is a kind of promise made by one party to the other, and honouring one's promises is the right thing to do. The second reason follows on from, and explains, the first. Fulfilling the conference agreement is strongly in the interests of all parties concerned. Non-fulfilment of agreement is one of the major causes of victim dissatisfaction and feelings of re-victimisation. At the very least, it creates feelings of disappointment and the suspicion that the offender was only faking their goodwill in the conference and that they really don't care.

When offenders do not fulfil agreements, other people feel let down and betrayed, and a negative rebound effect on the offenders may also be one of the results. If the offender fails to honour a promise, he or she may well experience a sense of shame or guilt, and feel the need to avoid those who have been let down. These feelings are likely to alienate the offender even further from the important people in his or her life, accelerating a downward slide into a criminal sub-culture. Thus, it should not surprise us that those offenders who do not honour their conference agreements are significantly more likely to re-offend than offenders who complete the tasks they agreed to.[1]

When contacting the offender and their supporters, ask them about progress to date towards fulfilling the agreement, and whether they can see any obstacles that would prevent completion on time. If there are difficulties, try to address them by enlisting the support of significant people in the offender's life, and inform the victim if modifications to the agreement are required. The only exception to this is when the victim does not wish to be informed. But even in these cases, it is important that the agreement is seen to completion, not least of all

---

1   Maxwell 1997.

because this is the most realistic way for the offender to free themselves of the burdens of their past conduct.

Finally, if the agreement is clearly not going to be honoured by the offender, then ensure that appropriate action is taken. This may mean reconvening the conference or, as a last resort, sending the case back to the police, or to court. Letting the matter slide would be the worst option in most cases, as it would only reinforce the offender's attitude of irresponsibility, which will not do them or anyone else any favours in the long run.

3. Informing conference participants of final disposition of the case.

All key stakeholders, and especially the victim, should be informed of successful completion of the conference agreement. This can be an important piece of knowledge to them in putting maters completely to rest. They should also be informed about non-completion of the agreement, of course. In cases where the conference is not going to be reconvened, stakeholders should be advised of the case being referred back to the police or to court, or whatever action has been decided by the conference convenor, or by their program. If you have a choice in the matter, you should not miss the chance to consult with the victim and the important people in the offender's life about what they may consider to be the best course of action. Consulting them will help them feel more in control of the situation in spite of non-completion of the agreement, and they are less likely to be left with a feeling that their involvement was a waste of time. Additionally, their input may enable you to make a more informed decision about what you should do next about the case.

6

FOR PARTICIPANTS: GENERAL COMMENTS

The most immediate aim of a restorative justice conference is to enable the offender to put things right with the victim. This is done by empowering both the victim and the offender, as well as their respective families and/or social support groups, to discuss and deal with the causes and the consequences of the incident in question as they see fit. As a participant, you should be aware of the distinction between primary and secondary stakeholders, and understand that it is the primary stakeholders that should be allowed to dominate the proceedings, rather than the other way around. The primary stakeholders are the people who have been the most directly involved in, and affected by, the wrongful behaviour in question, and it is they who must be supported and empowered to play active and decisive roles in the way the case is resolved. There may be cases, of course, where it is not immediately obvious whether you should think of yourself as a primary or secondary stakeholder, but that should not distract you from observing the principle behind the distinction, which is that the focus of attention should be commensurate to each participant's need for healing and restoration, and/or degree of responsibility for putting things right.

For the key parties to experience a sense of closure and healing, participants must be willing to speak from the heart, not merely from the mind. For you as a participant, whether as a primary or a secondary stakeholder, this means that you treat the incident essentially as a violation of a particular person, namely the victim, who was wronged and with whom matters need to be set right. All this requires going beyond discussions of relevant legal rights and obligations, as well as going beyond resolving the incident in strictly material terms. It requires exploration of how people were affected emotionally and what may be required to restore trust and peace between them. In the case of so-called victimless crimes, things will be somewhat different, since there are no readily identifiable persons who were harmed, in which case the harm may have been done to the common good, the local community, or to society in the most proper sense of the word.

General points for primary stakeholders

It follows from the above that, if you are a principal party, such as the primary victim, for example, or if the incident has affected you in a major way, it is important that you talk about the effects of the incident on you, not only materially, but also emotionally. This might mean, for example, talking about your sense of disappointment or personal violation and explaining how your sense of security, trust in other people, faith in human nature, etc, may have been affected as a result of this experience. The same holds true if you are the person responsible for the incident, or indeed a support person for either party. Along with your views about right and wrong, your feelings of disappointment, anger, indignation, resentment, shame, remorse etc, should be expressed in socially appropriate, non-abusive and non-violent ways as part of your contribution to the meeting. Such expressions have the most impact in a conference, as they convey to all those present the real significance of what happened. Without this, the others are less likely to respond to you in the most appropriate ways: they can only surmise what may be happening for you. To understand the impact of this incident on you, they must hear it for themselves directly from you.

Also, if you are a primary stakeholder in the case, then it should be you and the other main party who are the centre of the meeting, not only in terms of being the focus of attention, but more importantly, in the sense of taking a central role in what is being discussed. The role of everybody else in the conference, including legal advocates, agency representatives, and your own family and friends, is to lend you support in doing just that, and it is the facilitator's role to ensure that all of this does happen.

If you find yourself frustrated because you are not being heard or because others are dominating the conference discussion and are taking it in directions that are of little concern to you, then it is important that you signal this to the meeting. You are perfectly within your rights to verbalise your frustrations and suggest refocusing the discussion on the matters that are important to you. Alternatively, you should ask for time out to discuss matters with your family and other supporters, and/or the facilitator. A brief private session will give you a chance to express your concerns in a safe environment and get a wider perspective on them. Then it will be up to you whether you pursue those concerns when the conference reconvenes.

Of course, ultimately it is your choice to remain silent and let others do all the talking in your conference, but this will typically increase the chances of an unsatisfying experience and outcome for you and the other party. Especially if you are the offender, it is very important that you talk about the incident and accept fair responsibility for your behaviour. Your current attitude about what you did will be of major interest to everybody present. Attempts to rationalise wrongful behaviour is likely to be met with swift disapproval from the group. Generally, the expectation is that if you have done wrong, you should own up to it. Your honesty and courage in doing this will serve as the basis of respect which the others will gradually develop towards you in the course of the meeting. Their respect for you will further increase when you honour the conference agreement. If you remain disengaged during the conference, this process of establishing trust cannot begin and will be likely to frustrate the other participants who may respond with hostility.

But whether you are an offender or a victim, explaining how it looks and feels from your point of view is extremely important, not only for you to get things off your chest, but equally because it gives the other party and everybody else a chance to take you, and whatever matters to you, seriously and formulate an appropriate response. If in the end you are dissatisfied with the way things proceeded and were decided, the conference will have failed to achieve its primary objective. To prevent this from happening, the time for speaking up is in the conference. A good strategy is to note down before the conference a list of things you want to say, and of questions you want answered. Glancing at this list from time to time, and adding to it if new things occur to you as the conference develops, will ensure that you do not miss raising any of the issues that are important to you.

General points for secondary stakeholders

If you attend a conference as a secondary stakeholder (agency or legal representative, or supporter of either of the principal parties), then your proper role is to express your views on the matter honestly and openly when so requested, and generally lend support to the primary parties, helping and empowering them to deal with their issues the way it is best for *them*.

Should you have misgivings about the way things are going, or about the viability and indeed the fairness of the proposed agreement, it is very important that you state your concerns, but making it clear that you do not wish to impose your sense of right and wrong on the primary parties. The most important thing is that you express your views and draw the group's attention to details or concerns that may have escaped their attention. Then, having shared your concerns, the best thing you can do is let the primary parties decide how they wish to address them. There is, of course, often a need to engage in further discussion and clarifications, but the basic principle for you to observe here is that, ultimately, it is the parties who have the most at stake that must satisfy themselves about the rightness of the agreement. The primary stakeholders therefore must be given the opportunity and support to resolve the issues in a way that is right for *them* within the law.

Fearlessly expressing your sense of fairness to the meeting is very important. The power and efficacy of conferencing is precisely due to such down to earth, honest contributions. They also imbue the conference with stability in what, otherwise, could be a volatile situation. Even if the opinions and emotions of some participants are extreme, their excesses are quickly balanced by the moderating influence of more balanced and reasonable views expressed by other participants.

Having said that, it is the principal parties' views and interests that must prevail. The occasion has taken place primarily for *their* benefit, with *their* needs and interests in mind, and therefore, it is *they* who must feel satisfied with justice, or even with a compromise that falls short of complete justice. What must be kept in mind is that the primary aim of the conference is to enable the key participants to reach a sense of closure with respect to the incident, so that they can move on with their lives.

While no individual approach can be claimed to be fail-proof, the following chapters contain more detail on points that are likely to help you as a participant to maximise the chances of a successful conference. If nothing else, these points will help you avoid some of the most common pitfalls, which, even if committed inadvertently, can unnecessarily sour or jeopardise an otherwise attainable, positive outcome.

7

FOR VICTIMS
AND VICTIM SUPPORTERS

If you are a victim

Before the conference

1. Inform yourself beforehand of your rights and responsibilities under the relevant law(s), and generally find out about the legislation under which the conference is being convened.

The best sources of information in these regards are the conference coordinator and their agency. However, approaching specialist victim support groups is another option, as is, of course, talking to the police. It is also a good idea to talk to someone, such as a police officer who regularly attends conferences, and who may even be attending your particular conference, as they can give you a good idea of what usually happens and what you should be mindful of in preparing.

You should arm yourself with the knowledge of your legal rights and responsibilities. Such knowledge will provide you with the context within which your conference is going to take place. In some jurisdictions conferences have the status of police cautions, while in others they are convened under conference-specific legislation. The legal basis of the conference may have important implications for you in terms of your rights and options. For example, under New Zealand's *Children, Young Persons, and Their Families Act* 1989, victims have the right of veto, as do offenders, conference coordinators, and the Police. This means that a victim who is not satisfied with some proposed resolution in the conference can have the matter referred to court. However, to exercise this right, the victim must be present at the conference, or the other participants will deal with the matter as they see appropriate. Again, under the New South Wales *Young Offenders Act 1997*, victims have the right of veto, but the police do not, so you need to find out what laws apply in your jurisdiction.

2. Find out beforehand from your legal advocate, the police, or prosecutor, what the likely outcome would be if the matter was heard, instead, in court.

While such knowledge is often unnecessary for achieving satisfying conference outcomes, as a victim you will be placed in a much more powerful position for constructive negotiations in the conference if you have a realistic sense of what the alternatives are. At the very least, such knowledge will guard you from unnecessarily giving your consent to agreements with which you are clearly unhappy, or are likely to regret. If you would rather see the case decided in court, you should not miss exercising that option on account of being inadequately informed either about your legal rights, or about the likely outcome of the case in court. Keep in mind that going to court may well be a disincentive for the offender, as it is likely to result in a criminal conviction, which they otherwise might avoid having against their name.

3. If you were given inadequate notice, or the proposed time or venue don t suit you, ask and, if necessary, insist that the matter be rescheduled.

Should it be necessary to press the point, knowing your legal rights will prove helpful. It is likely to be one of your rights to be informed in good time about the conference. Even so, some coordinators neglect their responsibilities under the law towards victims, and victims must stand up for themselves if this happens. Do not let an uncooperative coordinator fob you off. Ask to speak to their manager, and if that fails, seek to discuss the matter with the police representative, who will be attending the conference. If the police have the right of veto, as in New Zealand, they may well choose to exercise their powers by insisting on reconvening the conference at a time that suits you and your support group.

4. Find out who else is going to be present at the conference, and organise a strong support group to attend with you.

Depending on how serious the case is, having with you four, five, six or more people for support is important. These should be the most important people in your life, typically family and close friends, the people you trust and respect the most. The important thing is for you to feel supported and safe in the conference. Unfortunately, early legislation on conferencing tends to specify only one other supporter of the victim's choice to be legally entitled to attend. Such laws are short-sighted, but conference convenors are typically happy to allow more supporters to attend. Those who do not are doing a disservice to themselves, the offender, and of course to you, the victim. However, not all conference coordinators have received adequate training in how to apply principles of restorative justice. The power of restorative justice conferencing is primarily dependent on bringing together strong, supportive people from both sides of the conflict. Potentially, this is more important than any other consideration, including skills of effective facilitation. This is because strong groups will invariably get down to the task at hand and will require little help in sorting matters out to everyone's satisfaction.

There is one very important point about selecting, inviting, and preparing your supporters for the conference: Your supporters should not be people who will experience conflicts of loyalty between you and the offender. While conferencing is not an adversarial process, the reality is that parties in the conference do not always see eye-to-eye with each other. Especially in the early stages of a conference there can be considerable tension until differences are sorted out. Therefore, at least some of your supporters should not only be loyal to you but also fearless in defending you and your interests, in the event that the offender proves unapologetic or otherwise difficult. Having with you such supporters is your insurance against being re-victimised or feeling intimidated in the conference.

While you and your supporters should avoid being unnecessarily aggressive and derogatory in your disagreements with other participants, your views about what is right or wrong must find clear expression and must figure prominently in discussions. If you do not have adequate support, or your supporters are too timid in voicing their objections about something they think is unfair, you may find yourself standing alone, wondering why you even bothered to come along, or worse. Such victim dissatisfaction does occur in a small percentage of cases in any program, and in some jurisdictions disconcertingly high rates of re-victimisation have been found.[1]

Should your supporters be in a position where their loyalties are divided between you and the offender, make especially sure that they are not going to desert you when you need them most. For example, in workplace conferences where the offender may be your, and their, boss or colleague, and more generally in conferences where your supporters expect regular interactions with the offender, they can find themselves

---

[1] For example, in the New Zealand Youth Justice Conferencing Program about one third of victims reported being revictimised, or feeling worse as a result of attending their FGC. (Maxwell & Morris 1993, 1996) These have been detailed in the Preface.

unable to stand up for you in the way you would need and expect them to, especially when disagreements arise.[2]

Suppose, for example, that the offender tries to rationalise or trivialise the seriousness of their behaviour and tries to shift some, or all, of the blame onto you. Will your supporters be able to tell the offender that they are wrong and that, instead of blaming you, they should own up and apologise for their wrongful behaviour? If it looks like your supporters might have difficulties answering this question with a clear "Yes," then you should check with them beforehand the degree of support you can realistically expect of them in the event that you end up in radical disagreement with the offender, who may be your, and their, friend, colleague, neighbour, or boss. Otherwise, there is a clear risk of finding yourself without support when you need it most.

If it looks like your support is shaky, you should check with the convenor about the general attitude of the offender and their support group. Provided their supporters have a healthy attitude towards what happened, the offender's attitude will not matter all that much. If they try to rationalise or trivialise their own behaviour, you will most probably find that their own supporters will come to your aid. This is not at all uncommon. However, if the available information suggests that both the offender and their supporters will be difficult to deal with, then you may still attend your conference, but should be prepared to weather any difficulties on your own. Alternatively, and only as a last resort, you may elect to be represented by somebody else, such as the police, or a professional victim support person. Having them along for support, however, is potentially preferable to you not attending.

Ultimately, however, not going ahead with a conference at all, but choosing alternative ways of resolving the issues must always be treated as live options. If you, as a victim, feel fragile and indications are that you are dealing with a very defensive group, while at the same time your own support group looks shaky, not risking exposure to further trauma may be advisable. While the general presumption should be in favour of attending your conference, you should always assess the risks of a bad experience in light of the considerations just discussed, and decide what is best for you.

---

2   Workplace conferences are especially likely to prove problematic, when the offender is a colleague or a boss and, instead of taking responsibility for their wrongful behaviour, they try to rationalise it or go on the attack. Because of the power imbalance, victims can find themselves standing on their own against their boss or an aggressive colleague, deserted by their own supporters who, for whatever reason, are hesitant to speak their minds in the meeting or come to the victim's defence. (See also the next section for Victim Supporters.)

5. *Find out about the facilitation process and, if appropriate, request changes to be made to it.*

Reading Chapter 4 again, which compares various facilitation processes, will help to appreciate the importance of this point. Indeed, you can request the facilitator to follow a process that you feel most comfortable with. To aid the facilitator, scripted prompts are provided in the Appendices. For example, you should check beforehand with the facilitator and request that the offender be asked to speak first, ideally to tell their story and express their view about how they see their own actions at the present moment.

However, if the offender is unable or unwilling to speak, the wrongdoer's close supporters should be asked to speak first, explaining what may be happening to the (silent) offender, and expressing their own moral views about the matter. There may also be cultural reasons for deviating from the general preference for giving the offender first say in the process. In some cultural contexts, it would be inappropriate for a young offender to talk about the offence (first), or to negotiate a resolution with the victim. The custom may be that it is their family who is supposed to do the talking in such situations. In some cultures it is considered rude for a young person to speak before, or instead of, the adults in their family, and these should be allowed for in a conference.

During the conference

1. Give the wrongdoer and their family an opportunity to speak first.

Unless this has already been arranged, you can ask them to tell in detail of the events leading up to the incident and of the offence itself, as well as their *reasons* for doing what they did. In all fairness, it is the facilitator who should prompt the offender to do all this, but you cannot always, and indeed need not, rely on them to ensure that these things happen in the meeting.

But, regardless of how it is achieved, the point here is that it is typically best for you and everybody else, if from the very start you gain insight into the offender's actions, motivations, and current attitude to what they did. Hearing the offender recounting their own wrongful actions is typically a very revealing experience, and their attitudes to what they did will probably have a major impact on what you think of them and the way you will want to see the situation resolved. As explained earlier, if you or the police officer speak first, it increases the likelihood of the offender not revealing themselves honestly, or worse, their attitude can turn for the worse, which will result in aggravation for everyone involved. This danger will be less likely if the wrongdoer is asked to speak first.

Whether you then have second say, or you want to hear the offender's supporters views before you speak, is less important, but it is a good idea to hear early on the views and attitudes of the offender's whole family and social support group present. This will help you understand better why things turned out the way they did, whether the offence was out of character, or whether there are deeper problems in the offender's family and social environment. All this extra information will enable you to pitch your participation and contribution in an informed way for maximum effect.

2. *If still unclear, when your turn comes ask the wrongdoer to say how they feel about what they have done, and especially about the consequences of their behaviour for you. Similarly, find out from the wrongdoer s supporters how they see the same.*

Few offenders remain unaffected by their own wrongful behaviour. The mere fact that they have been caught doing the wrong thing sets off a process of thinking, and they are most unlikely to feel pleased with themselves about the trauma they have caused to others. Feeling bad about hurting the victim is something that can almost be taken for granted about the vast majority of offenders, even if at the time of the offence they were unconcerned about such matters. Understanding is often gained with hindsight, and this is generally true of behaviour that wrongfully harms others. Therefore, to gain a proper understanding of the current situation and to judge it accurately, it is important to judge it in light of the evolution that the offender's attitude may have undergone since the time of the incident. For the very same reasons, it is important to find out how the wrongdoer's supporters see the matter.

3. *If you see the offender behave in inappropriate ways, such as smiling and laughing, do not assume that they feel proud about what they did. Ask them about it.*

You will probably find that they are doing this out of nervousness, and that they are unaware of what they are doing and of the effect it has on the other participants. Once their attention is drawn to it, the behaviour usually stops.

4. *When your turn comes, tell the conference how this incident affected you, taking into account any new understanding you may have gained from the other party s contributions.*

Speak boldly; say it how it is. Do not hold back either your opinions or emotions, but do express them in socially acceptable (non-violent and preferably non-abusive) ways. This will enable the other participants to gain a good understanding of your situation. Expressions of indignation and anger are perfectly in place, as is crying. Be yourself. If you are genuine, others will spontaneously copy you and will respond in the same way. If you think that some proposal is unfair or unsatisfactory from your point of view, you should say so. Only this will allow others a chance to address your concerns.

5. *At the start of negotiating an agreement, and before putting forward your own views and requests for appropriate reparation, ask the offender (and/or their family), whether there was anything in particular that they would like to say or do by way of putting things right.*

Once again, it is the facilitator who should initiate negotiations with this approach, but relatively few facilitators have been trained to do so. Most frequently they will start this stage of the conference by asking you, the victim, to say what you would like to see happen. If this happens, you can give the offender a chance to mention any initiative or plan they might have. You will then be better placed to judge their view of the situation, and can put forward your own ideas and expectations in a more informed way. If what is being offered is inadequate, you should say so, and give reasons for your views. The other party then will have a chance to respond to your views, and so on, until you reach a mutually satisfactory agreement.

6. *If you think that an apology from the wrongdoer would be in place, say so at an appropriate moment.*

A good time for this is shortly before, or at the start of, negotiations for an agreement. The wrongdoer may simply have forgotten to apologise, especially if they feel overwhelmed by the conference. Most often, however, they will take the opportunity to apologise, especially if they are given the opportunity, such as when being asked whether there is anything they wanted to say or do to put things right.

7. *During negotiations, articulate clearly your views on what you would consider a fair agreement or resolution.*

It is your right to see justice done, provided your proposals are within the law. It is also your prerogative to season the legitimate claims of justice with forgiveness and mercy. Do whatever feels right for you. Remember that this is *your* day, and that, for better or worse, it is *you* who will have to live with the final agreement and/or outcome.

8. Be assertive about the things that are important to you.

Do not let anybody (such as the facilitator, other professionals, or even your own supporters) push you around. You do not have to agree to anything that does not feel right to you. Doing so will only make it harder for you to put matters to rest.

After the conference

1. If you would like to know whether the conference agreement is being fulfilled, ask to be informed.

This is your right.

2. If the agreement is not fulfilled, you are entitled to an explanation and an appropriate remedy to the situation. You can ask that the conference be reconvened.

It is always a good idea to have the conference re-convened so that you can get your questions answered and satisfy yourself as to the situation. Alternatively, you can ask the matter to be dealt with by court. The first option is the most desirable one. It sometimes takes several attempts to bring about lasting change in someone's life, and this may be true of your offender. But if you do not wish to meet with the offender again, try everything within reason to ensure that the case is at least taken to court. Inaction would only reinforce an attitude of irresponsibility in the wrongdoer, whereby nobody wins, least of all the wrongdoer.

In the event that the agreement is not fulfilled, the case may be referred to court as a matter of course. Even so, it is a good idea to discuss with the police the possibility of obtaining fair compensation or reparation for the losses you suffered, and they may be able to represent your material interests at the hearing. Also, in many jurisdictions there are support groups for victims of crime who can give you the necessary information and support.

If you are a support person for the victim

If you are a parent or a guardian of an underage victim, then this chapter speaks to you. But even if you are supporting an adult, you are still encouraged to read this chapter.

There is, however, one point that must be emphasised for victim supporters. This concerns the difficulties created by occasional conflicts of loyalty that you may experience between the offender and the victim. As pointed out in the previous section, this is most likely in workplace conferences and more generally in conferences where you expect to continue to interact with the offender. Suppose, for example, that the offender decides to rationalise or trivialise the seriousness of what they did and tries to shift blame to the victim. Will you be able and willing to tell the offender that they are wrong and that, instead of blaming others, they should own up and apologise?

If you hesitate answering with a clear "Yes," then you should clarify with the victim the degree of support you can realistically lend them if they end up in a radical disagreement with the offender, who may be their, and your, friend, colleague, neighbour, or boss. Otherwise, there is a risk of the victim finding themselves alone when they need their supporters most. It is not easy, of course, to tell somebody with whom you agree and sympathise that you are unable to defend them publicly. But it is far worse to oblige the victim by going along as a supporter, hoping that everything will go smoothly, and then finding yourself torn between incompatible loyalties, and failing to support the victim when they need your support most.

8

FOR OFFENDERS
AND OFFENDER SUPPORTERS

If you are an offender
Before the conference

1. *Inform yourself beforehand about your rights and responsibilities under the relevant law(s), and generally find out about the law under which the conference is being convened.*

The best sources of information in these regards are the conference coordinator and their agency. Discussing the matter with your legal advocate is another option, but beware of an overly legalistic framing of the situation, or worse, an outright adversarial approach to the conference.

Unlike in court, where it is expected of your lawyer to try everything possible to minimise your responsibility and help you get the lightest possible penalty by fair means or foul, this kind of approach is totally counter-productive in a conference and it will unnecessarily upset a lot of people, hindering your interests in settling matters with the victim and putting them behind you. You will be expected to forget about legal technicalities and own up honestly to what you have done wrong, without making excuses or trying to minimise your responsibility in any way. This takes courage, and you may feel vulnerable, but you will earn respect, as well as start earning the trust of everyone present.

Trust is the foundation of reconciliation, and without taking responsibility for the wrongdoing, building trust will be difficult, as your sincerity, good will, and even whether you care about having hurt others, will remain in question in the other participants' minds, not least the victim's. Therefore, if you are going to talk to a lawyer, it is a good idea to talk to one who regularly attends conferences.

You may also want to have your lawyer with you at the conference, but their role there should be to observe proceedings to ensure that your rights are protected. While they will be included in the discussions at appropriate times, it would be most unhelpful if they did the talking for you in the way they would in court. Like everybody else, you will be expected to speak for yourself, and you will do best if your primary focus is on taking full responsibility for your actions and then offering to do whatever is required, within reason, to put things right with the victim. This is the best way for you to demonstrate to everyone present that you are "not such a bad person, after all". A conference that starts on such a constructive note is well on the way to being a success.

Having said that, you should nevertheless empower yourself with the knowledge of your legal rights and responsibilities. Such knowledge provides you with the overall context within which your conference is going to take place. In some jurisdictions, conferences have the status of police cautions, while in others they are convened under conference-specific legislation.

If you would rather see the case being decided in court, you should not miss exercising that option on account of being inadequately informed about your legal rights. If this is a diversionary conference, you can elect to have your case heard in court at any point, before, during, and even after the conference. Conference is not your only option, so do not feel obliged or pressured into it, if you feel that you are not getting a fair hearing or treatment.

2. Find out beforehand who in your conference will have the right of veto.

The right of veto means that if someone who has this right is not satisfied with the proposed resolution, they have the legal power to see the matter being settled in court. The power of veto can change from jurisdiction to jurisdiction. Under New Zealand's *Children, Young Persons, and Their Families Act* 1989, for example, proposed agreements may be vetoed by the victim, the offender, the conference coordinator, and the Police, whereas under the NSW *Young Offenders Act* 1995 the police elected not to be granted that power. This means that police cannot veto an agreement, not even on behalf of a victim and, unlike in New Zealand, they often choose not to be present at conferences.

3. Find out from your legal advocate what the likely outcome would be if the matter were to be sent to court.

With such knowledge, you will be placed in a much better position for constructive negotiations. At the very least, such knowledge will guard you from unnecessarily giving your consent to agreements with which you are unhappy, or are likely to regret. Most importantly, finding out about the likely outcome of a court case can save you from pleading guilty to, or admitting responsibility for, things you have not done. While denying responsibility just because you can get away with it would be wrong, it would be equally wrong of you to admit responsibility for things you are not responsible for, just because this will give you a conference and save you from having to defend yourself in court.

4. *If you were given inadequate notice, or the proposed time or venue don t suit you, ask and, if necessary, insist that the matter be rescheduled.*

Should you find it necessary to press the point, knowing your legal rights will prove helpful.

5. *Find out who else is going to be present at the conference, and organise a strong support group to attend the conference with you.*

Depending on how serious the case is, having with you four, five, six or more people for support is important. These should be the most important people in your life, typically family and close friends and peers, the people whom you trust and respect most. They should be people who you can rely on and who will not hesitate to defend you against clearly unreasonable demands. They should also be the people who will not bully you into things you don't agree with. Sometimes bullying can be more of a danger from your own supporters than from the victim or the police. The most important thing is for you to feel supported and safe in attending the conference. Keep firmly in mind, however, that your confidence and support group should not be used for doing battle with the victim, the police, or anybody else – unless, of course, they are clearly unreasonable – but for being able to find your voice and stand your ground in terms of taking responsibility for your behaviour. This means admitting what you did wrong, and indicating a genuine intention to put things right with the victim.

Your supporters should back you up in doing this. Their expressions of respect for you and confidence in you will also bolster your credibility with the other party and with the relevant third parties. To a large extent, your credibility and character will be judged on the kind of person you show yourself to be at the conference, but their judgment of the situation will be influenced just as much by the kind of people you have with you as supporters and the kind of support your supporters give you. Of course, if you have been continuously in trouble with the law, your own family may be frustrated, angry, and losing confidence in you. But if you care about winning back their confidence and respect, you may be surprised by how easily and quickly this can happen in a conference once your family sees you taking responsibility for your behaviour and wanting to do the right thing by the victim.

6. *Think seriously about offering an apology to those who have been affected by your actions, and about practical ways of repairing the harm.*

Typically, a conference is not only about what you have done, but even more importantly about the kind of person you are, and want to be. Nobody is infallible; we all make mistakes. This seems to be implicitly recognised in conferences, and therefore, while initial discussion will concern mostly the incident in question, you should expect that, as the conference proceeds, there will be a lot of interest shown in what *kind of person* you are and want to be. This, in turn, will be judged by your attitude to your own wrongful behaviour, and especially by whether it was out of character, and your sense of fairness, and courage to admit that it was wrong and that it should be put right.

Offering an apology from the very outset is unlikely to earn you instant forgiveness, but it will demonstrate to the other participants that you are the kind of person who cares about how others have been affected. Putting some thought into additional ways of putting things right with the victim will serve the same function. Your goodwill is going to serve as the foundation of building trust and possibly a true and lasting reconciliation.

The beginning of a conference is the most appropriate time to offer an apology and again just before moving on to start working out the conference agreement. Offering restitution in more practical ways tends to be most appropriate at the start of the Agreement stage of the conference. These suggestions about timing are only rules of thumb, however. You should use every opportunity for apologising and offering to make amends. Your suggestions may be modified and may not even remain as part of the final agreement, but that is neither here nor there. The main point is that, if you have put some thought into how to make things right with the victim, this should be evident at the conference. It will accelerate the process of establishing mutual trust and respect between you and the other participants, and is likely to result in an easier conference than would be the case otherwise.

7. *Find out about the facilitation process and, if appropriate, request changes to be made to it.*

Re-reading Chapter 4, which compares various facilitation processes, will be helpful in appreciating the importance of this point. Indeed, you can request the convenor to follow a process that you feel most comfortable with.

You should make a point of requesting that you and/or your family be allowed to speak first, so that you can start off the conference on a positive note, acknowledging your responsibility and possibly offering your apologies to those adversely affected by the incident, and assuring everybody of your goodwill. However, if you are unable or not confident enough to speak first, then one of your close supporters should be allowed to say those things on your behalf. This may also be the more culturally appropriate way to proceed. The other participants are unlikely to object, provided that it is briefly explained to them.

During the conference

8. *Unless otherwise required by your own culture, and unless this has already been arranged with the facilitator, ask to be allowed to speak first.*

You should start by briefly stating the way you have come to see your own actions since the incident (whether it was right or wrong). If you think that an apology is appropriate, take this opportunity to apologise to the victim and everybody else who has been affected by what you did. It would be unrealistic to expect that you will be instantly forgiven. However, a sincere apology will have a calming effect on the meeting and will build trust and sooth hard feelings. Trust, however, is most likely to be acquired gradually. Depending on the nature and seriousness of the offence, it may not be until after the conference that any signs of conciliation and forgiveness will be forthcoming from the victim. The best policy for you is not to expect it. If, and when, it happens, it will be a gift.

Immediately after apologising and indicating your desire to make amends, offer to answer any questions about yourself and what happened. In all fairness, it is the facilitator who should prompt you to do all this, but you cannot always, and indeed need not, rely on them to ensure that all the important things are dealt with adequately. But, regardless of whether the facilitator prompts you in this way, the point here is that it is typically best for you and everybody else, if you can start off the conference on such a positive and constructive note. Chances are that this will have a major impact on what the victim and the meeting will think of you, and on the way they will want to see the matter resolved. As explained earlier, if you let the police officer or the victim speak first, the chances of a maximally restorative experience are unnecessarily diminished and the meeting can result in considerable aggravation for everybody involved. This can be avoided if you have a chance of starting off on a conciliatory note.

9. Be patient with an upset and angry victim. Allow them to take their time to work through their grief and the anger they have towards you.

A typical conference, where issues are addressed in proper detail, and where strong representation is present from both sides, will last between two to three hours. Sometimes the victim will not be able to get over their hurt in such a short time. If the hurt or the loss has been particularly great, it may never happen at all. That, however, does not mean that they will not benefit from having met you and talked to you, and it certainly should not stop you from doing the right thing by apologising and offering to comply with suggestions they might have for putting things right or at least making it better for them.

If the victim continues to be angry with you in spite of all your efforts, bear with them, and let them be. It is likely that others will come to your aid. It is wise to let others speak up on your behalf to defend you as a good person, if they are willing. Hence the importance of having reasonable and courageous supporters with you.

The danger in trying to defend yourself is that it will be taken as defiance and lack of remorse. Even if this is a mistaken perception, it will be likely to upset a lot of people. There is room here, perhaps, for you to be philosophical about it. If your initial actions were out of place and have caused distress and harm to others, it may not be entirely unfair if you choose to endure a bit of a hard time from those people. You should never give up your right, however, to be treated with fairness.

10. Even though you can expect to feel nervous and anxious in a conference, try to stay calm, and listen closely to what people say.

Fidgeting, being distracted, and smiling out of nervousness are likely to be interpreted by others that you are not treating the matter with the kind of seriousness it deserves. This will hinder the process of conciliation. If you are challenged about something like this, simply apologise and explain that you are just nervous (if, indeed, that is the case). Try to maintain good eye contact with people when they talk to you. To stop continuous nervous activity, clutch your hands together and lock your feet, if you have to. Otherwise, you are likely to be seen to be uninterested and not wanting to be there. Even if in some sense this may be true, you should avoid aggravating the meeting with unconscious nervous activity. If it is culturally inappropriate for you to look people in the eye when talking to them, then this should be explained to the group at the meeting, possibly by one of your adult supporters, or the facilitator who should be advised about it beforehand.

11. *At the start of negotiating an agreement, take the opportunity to let the victim and the meeting know that you have been thinking about ways of putting things right. Tell them what you have been thinking about.*

Once again, it is the facilitator who should offer you this opportunity at the start of negotiations by asking you whether there was anything you might like to say, or whether there was anything you thought of doing to put things right. Although a facilitator may not have been trained to commence negotiations this way, they can easily accommodate such requests. Many of them have been trained to start this stage of the conference by asking the victim to say what they would like to see happen. If this happens, listen carefully to what the victim says. In your response, take the opportunity to mention any plan that you might have thought about as being among the possibilities. Then let the meeting consider the fairness and feasibility of the various options. If what is being suggested is unfeasible or unfair from your point of view, you should not hesitate to say so, giving your reasons but indicating your openness to other suggestions for putting things right. The others then will have a chance to respond to your views, and so on, until you reach a mutually satisfactory agreement.

12. *Be assertive about the things that are important to you.*

Do not let anybody (such as, the facilitator, other professionals, or even your own supporters) push you around, and do not agree to anything that does not feel right to you. If you are unable to speak up about your concerns, ask for a brief private session to discuss the matter with your supporters. It is most important that you are satisfied with the outcome. If you are unhappy with the agreement because you feel strongly that it is unfair, the conference will have failed you in an important area. If, however, you are alone in objecting to the proposed agreement, then you might have to re-assess the situation to see if there was something that you missed. It can also happen that you are not completely happy with the agreement, but since you can live with it, you decide to satisfy the victim and the other parties, so that the matter can be put to rest.

Such compromises are acceptable, provided that you don't feel that the agreement is grossly unfair, and something that you are going to resent. That clearly would not constitute a case of putting matters behind you, which was supposed to be one of the key objectives of the exercise.

After the conference

1. Ensure that you fulfil your obligations under the conference agreement.[1] If this becomes unfeasible, or if you think that the agreement is grossly unfair, then you must contact the convenor to discuss the issue and possibly arrange for the conference to be re-convened.

If the matter is minor, appropriate changes to the agreement can be negotiated with the convenor, who can consult and check with the victim. If sorting out the problem seems difficult or complicated, then a review conference should be convened as soon as possible, especially if you feel strongly that the agreement is too unfair for you to comply with. This can happen, and it is one of the reasons why it is so important that you do not allow yourself to be pushed into things when you don't agree with them, and also why you should have a strong support group with you. Sometimes, unfortunately, it will be your own supporters who will prove the most overbearing in a conference, especially if you are a young person. But whatever happened in the conference, the point is that if you have agreed to a certain resolution, then you have given your word and made a promise that morally binds you to fulfil that agreement. Therefore, if you are not going to fulfil the agreement for any reason, you need to inform the relevant people about it and negotiate alternative arrangements.

This may or may not require another conference, but if you do not take the initiative to inform people and raise your concerns, and choose instead to ignore the promise you made, it will reflect badly on you and will cause a lot of people to be disappointed in you, once again. Rightly or wrongly, the assumption will be that you are irresponsible after all, and that your remorse and decency at the conference were feigned. In the absence of a credible explanation, victims and others will assume that they have been duped, and that you are, after all, the kind of person who is too selfish to care about doing the right thing by other people. Thus, an unexplained failure to fulfil the conference agreement is likely to undo most of the progress made by you and the other participants towards reconciliation. Unfulfilled agreements are one of the main causes of victims feeling re-victimised, and doubts about your good will and moral integrity will not be far from your own supporters' and family's minds. Moreover, your failure to take appropriate action is

---

1   Provided, of course, that there was an agreement. Post-court conferences, for example, typically are not intended to result in formal agreements. They are convened for purposes of facilitating closure, reconciliation and healing for the parties involved after the case was dealt with in court. These typically concern very serious offences, such as armed robbery, assault, manslaughter and murder.

likely to cause them further embarrassment. Thus, it is imperative that an agreement that is not going to be honoured is not ignored by you, but is re-negotiated with the appropriate parties.

It is a good idea to have the conference re-convened so that you can explain your reasons, especially if you do not wish to fulfil the agreement because you think it is unfair. If you do not find satisfaction with the group, you should ask that the matter be dealt with by court. Indeed, in the event that there is no agreement, or if the agreement is not fulfilled, the case is likely to be referred to court as a matter of course. Even if you wanted this to happen, not having taken any action about an unfulfilled agreement will not speak well of you before the court. If you wish the matter to proceed to court, you should request it, rather than being brought before the court by others for failing to honour your word and commitment.

If you are a support person for the offender

If you are a parent or guardian of an underage offender, then this chapter speaks directly to you. But even if you are a supporter of an adult offender, you are strongly encouraged to read this chapter, as well as the previous and following chapters, as these will provide you with a good understanding of the proper roles of the various participants and what you can reasonably expect of them.

As explained earlier, the conference should start with the offender having first say. Sometimes, however, the offender may not be able or willing to do it. In such a case, a close supporter should take the initiative and start the conference on a conciliatory note. For example, even if you are not the one responsible for the harm to the victim, you can still express regret over the situation and assure them that in your view the incident was not their fault. This is important for the victim, and it is the right thing to do, especially if the offender is detached, defiant, and appears not to care. Healing and reconciliation are still possible, and indeed are very likely between the two sides, even if the offender is unable or unwilling to be part of it.

On the other hand, if the offender feels too frightened or embarrassed to talk, then an offender supporter should explain this to the meeting and speak on their behalf, offering an apology and a brief account of how the offender feels about what they did and what has happened in their life since the incident. Doing this from the start will help prevent the other party from assuming the worst about the offender. A conciliatory gesture such as this will quickly establish the right tone for the conference.

When the time comes for working out a conference agreement, lend whatever support you can to the offender. As explained earlier, it is a good idea to think of something beforehand, so that the goodwill of your group becomes even more apparent to the victim and the other participants. Therefore, it would be of great benefit to raise these matters with the offender before the conference. Apart from making them feel strongly supported, this kind of approach will also have the benefit of providing the offender with a positive role model, an example of the kind of attitude that is appropriate to take towards one's mistakes and wrongful actions.

Another very important role of offender supporters is to ensure that the conference agreement is both fair and achievable, and that, once agreed to, it is fulfilled. If the agreement is not honoured, a lot of the progress made by both parties will be undone. The offender's sincerity and character will be once again in question and participants will feel that they were being lied to and were duped in the conference. Also, rather than feeling the additional burden of a broken promise, honouring the conference agreement will give the offender a sense of release in the knowledge that the mistakes of the past have been addressed. A liberating feeling from the troubles and burdens of the past is a powerful impetus for a fresh start, both socially and psychologically. Being praised and congratulated for fulfilling their promise and putting things right with the victim will reinforce their commitment to doing the right thing in the future. This provides a powerful reason for holding a review conference with the victim who will be likely to be pleased to express their appreciation and respect for the offender for having done the right thing, and give them their best wishes for the future.

It is even more important, of course, to have a review conference in the event that the agreement is not fulfilled, so that problems can be examined afresh and remedied as appropriate – another obvious area where your support will be needed. As mentioned, non-fulfilment of agreement should be a rare occurrence, provided that the agreement was both fair and realistic, and that it was reached though a transparent, democratic process.

Being a support person for the offender is a difficult role, as it demands a fine act of balancing competing moral and emotional demands. On the one hand, the person whom you are there to support is in trouble. He or she needs your support and respect in facing the animosity and the anger of the people they have hurt. At the same time, condoning the wrongful behaviour of loved ones would be to embrace the kind of moral tribalism which may already have been a contributing factor behind the offence and the current crisis. To condone the wrongful behaviour of others would itself be wrong. Instead of resolving the crisis, it would only succeed in deepening it.

The challenge, then, is to disapprove of the offender's wrongful behaviour, while at the same time upholding the intrinsic moral worth of the offender as a person. This means that condemnation of their wrongful behaviour must be complemented by clear affirmations of their personal worth and importance as a valuable member of their family and community, and indeed of the wider moral community that makes up civil society. This kind of differentiation of the actor from the act is essential for securing maximally restorative outcomes, especially for the offender, but also for the victim and everybody else who has been affected. It clearly falls on you, the offender supporters, to lead the way in dealing with the situation in this fashion.

While in the abstract this may seem difficult, in practice it can be relatively simple, and it will come fairly easily, once the concept is understood and fears about telling a loved one that they have done wrong and that better behaviour is expected of them in the future are overcome. Here are some examples of the types of comments that are frequently heard in successful conferences from offender supporters:

> I do not approve of what John did. It was a stupid thing to do, and it is unfortunate that he had to learn it the hard way. But he remains a good friend to me, and I know that he is not going to do anything like this again.

> Mary used to be a responsible and well-behaved kid. I don't understand why over the past 12 months she has been so difficult. I have tried everything but she doesn't listen to me anymore. She seems to think that I am her enemy, and that really hurts me. I am her mother and I only want what is good for her. Even when she does a terrible thing like this, I cannot stop loving her, or being worried about her. She is my child. I worry myself sick and lie awake at night, not knowing where she is, what she does, and whether she is safe. I sometimes blame myself for the way she is, and I feel responsible for what she does. I pray that something can be done before something really terrible happens.

> I have known Peter since he was a young boy. I have always liked him, and I think that he is a smart kid with plenty of energy and imagination. But what he did is clearly unacceptable and must be put right. I also hope that he will never do anything like this again. Perhaps there is a lesson in this for us adults as well. We must be more vigilant and active in channelling youthful talent and energy. I certainly would like to do that with Peter, and I came with him today to help him sort this matter out with the people he hurt.

Comments and contributions like these are the essence of what Braithwaite calls 're-integrative shaming.'[2] They are shaming because the offender's behaviour is disapproved of, and they are re-integrative because the dignity, value, and the importance of the individual person is affirmed at the same time. Showing respect to the offender is like extending a hand towards them to remain in, or re-join, the community of moral and law-abiding citizens. As already explained, this kind of shaming is the antithesis of stigmatising or disintegrative shaming, which Braithwaite explicitly warns against. Such destructive forms of shaming can be seen in the following comments.

> You are a good for nothing. This is terrible. See what you have done?

> It is simply incredible. You are nothing but a bully.

> You are the shame of this family. What is wrong with you? Why can't you be normal like other people?

> You must be a sick person to do something like this.

The disappointment, disgust and the powerful feelings of shame and anger that typically lie behind comments such as these are entirely understandable, and in some sense are even justified. However, they are less likely to break through the protective shell of the offender in terms of eliciting a positive response and long-term change than are the type of reintegrative disapprovals quoted earlier. Instead, they are more likely to crush the offender's self-image as a valuable member of society. Such comments are also likely to make an offender feel rejected or victimised. Such attacks on them are most likely to lead to increased defensiveness, which will inhibit their ability to empathise with and care about the victim, or indeed about anything that the conference is trying to achieve. The need to maintain self-esteem is powerful, and a person whose worth is under attack will be less and less likely to empathise and respond positively to the concerns of their attackers. Short of being crushed, such stigmatising comments, especially from their own supporters, the people whose opinions they value most, leave them with no option but to reject their rejecters, leading to increased alienation and worsening forms of victimisation of others in the wider community, a community with which they can no longer identify.

Therefore, as an offender supporter, do not hesitate to say positive things about the offender. Indeed, it is crucial that you boost their confidence with positive, reintegrative comments. As long as it is clear

---

2   As discussed in Chapter 3.

that you do not condone their wrongful behaviour, your support for the offender will not cause distress to the victim and will not be considered inappropriate by the other participants. Indeed, such positive support for the offender will be expected by the other participants, who otherwise will start to suspect that the offender's problems originate from an unsupportive, uncaring family and social environment. Provided that the offender does not rationalise their behaviour, or trivialise its seriousness, the victim and the other participants will take their cues from you. They will gradually adopt the same kind of reintegrative framing of the situation and of the incident as you do when you condemn the wrongful act while affirming the value of the erring person.

You will be placed in a much more difficult position, of course, if the offender tries to justify their behaviour, or trivialises its seriousness, or worse, insinuates that the victim was in some way to blame. This typically arouses indignation and draws angry criticism from the other participants. The pressure is greatest on offender supporters at this point. Condoning the attitude of the offender towards their wrongdoing would be wrong in itself, as it would leave the offender's distorted perceptions unchallenged and because it would deny the victim the kind of validation they need and deserve from the offender and their supporters. Yet, if you challenge the offender on their attitude, you may alienate them altogether, leaving them with little to lose.

Notwithstanding such risk, your first duty to everyone at the conference, including the offender, is honesty about the way you see matters. Just as before, this need not involve, indeed it should not involve a rejection of the offender as a worthwhile person, child, brother, or friend. Disagreement with their poor attitude to what they did can be done in constructive, non-stigmatising ways in the manner already discussed. Such disapproval of deficient attitudes will validate the victim and will serve as food for thought for the offender after the conference. Without such honest feedback from the important people in their lives, they would have little chance of correcting their distorted sense of right and wrong.

9

FOR PROFESSIONALS

If you are a legal advocate for the offender

Unlike in the established tradition of the court, where you are expected to represent and speak for your client, the most constructive way for you to approach a conference is in an advisory role. Your main aim should be to empower your client, the offender, with the knowledge of their legal rights and a realistic appreciation of the likely outcome if the case were to be sent to court. They should have a good grasp of the advantages and disadvantages of having the case heard in court, as compared with having it conferenced, so that they can make an informed decision about which way they should proceed. As a general rule, unless your client is innocent, in which case they should be pleading not guilty, conference should prove preferable to court by a long margin. Conferencing allows, indeed requires, a cooperative, non-adversarial approach to resolving the matter, which is more likely to result in client satisfaction with justice all round. Successful conferencing, however, is premised on the involvement and empowerment of the primary stakeholders, and therefore you should encourage clients to speak for themselves in their conferences and take responsibility for making amends.

As explained in Chapter 2, this requires a moral approach to framing the problem, as opposed to a legalistic one. While it is particularly important that you do express your views and concerns in the event that your client's rights are in danger of being violated, or if you feel that they are being victimised and treated unfairly in any way, you should resist the temptation to take over the case in dealing with the other party. This would only turn the conference into another type of disempowering process by a third party, which is most likely to undermine its restorative potential for the key participants, in which case the matter could just as well have gone to court.

If you are a police officer or prosecutor

In some jurisdictions, such as in New Zealand and South Australia, you are given first say in the conference. Typically, this means reading out the official charges to the offender and asking them whether they admit or deny the charges. For the reasons already given, it is preferable to ask the offender, instead, to talk first about what they did and how they see their behaviour. You can then ask questions of them and clarify any details that may be at odds with the official charges, which may need minor amendments.

You will most likely find that this way of proceeding allows you and the other participants a much better picture of the offence and the events that led to it, which in turn will be important for finding adequate responses to it, not least of all in order to minimise the chances of its recurrence. This is important for everybody concerned. Beyond this point, your participation should be in a supportive role to the primary stakeholders and their respective families and support groups. They should be encouraged to discuss the incident as a moral matter in which the victim was hurt, rather than merely as a legal matter where the offender must answer to the state, with the police as its representative. This kind of moral approach, whereby the focus is on how crime affects people, rather than it being seen merely as a violation of the law, applies equally to you when it is your turn to share your views about the offence in the meeting. This was discussed in detail in Chapter 2.

When the time comes to working out an agreement, primary stakeholders must be allowed and encouraged to reach their own agreements, without undue influence or pressure from third parties, such as the police. This is quite compatible with your role as a servant and guardian of the public interest. Resolutions and agreements that make the key parties to the conflict happy will best serve society's interest in deterrence. If there is a strong victim representation present and they are all happy with some proposed resolution, then it would be wrong of the police and any other third party to overrule their wishes. It would undermine the very aim of the meeting to empower the primary stakeholders to deal with the matter within the law in a way that is right for them.

Such disempowerment of both the victim and the offender took place, for example, in the *Clotworthy* case, discussed in Chapter 1. In this case, the New Zealand Court of Appeal sent an offender to gaol against the wishes of the primary victim. After discussing the matter with the offender in a conference, the victim considered imprisonment to be a wasteful and inappropriate way to resolve the matter. Instead, the offender undertook to pay the victim's medical bills by remaining employed. With some modifications, the District Court approved the agreement and the matter was settled to everyone's satisfaction, except the Crown's, which subsequently succeeded in overturning the agreement in the Court of Appeal. From a restorative justice point of view, this was clearly wrong. The point in restorative justice is to facilitate the active involvement of primary stakeholders during all stages of the case and for them to make all the important decisions.

Decisions such as this demonstrate the dangers and consequences of disempowering primary stakeholders in restorative justice meetings.[1] But even more unacceptable are cases where third parties, including police, participate in fixing conference outcomes beforehand. This tends to happen in collaboration with other professionals, such as social workers, community representatives and the convenor, who decide on an "appropriate" outcome before the conference. Such collusion, thankfully, does not appear to be widespread. But when it does occur, it leaves the individuals and families involved deceived and redundant, as their decision-making powers have effectively been divested from them. Such practices are not only wrong, but outright illegal. Professionals who engage in such practices bring the justice system and their respective organisations into disrepute. Police are no exception. Even if nobody makes a formal complaint, many people will come to know about such underhanded practices and will not think well of those indulging in them.

Finally, there is a very important role that police must play at conferences – that is to provide a feeling of safety and security to the participants. As a police officer you need to be aware of the potentially coercive and threatening nature of your presence in a conference. This can be used for both positive and negative effect. For example, it can be used to support otherwise poorly supported and clearly vulnerable individuals, be they the offender, or the victim. You should not hesitate to come to their defence should you observe them coming under undue pressure or intimidation from aggressive, defiant or otherwise

---

1   McElrea 1996, 1999.

misguided participants. But you must also be careful not to intimidate an already timid, fearful, and shaken offender. It can happen that they cannot even find their voice in the conference, which helps no one.

If you are a social worker

As a secondary stakeholder, you can make the most difference in a restorative justice conference by aiding the creation and empowerment of strong families and communities of care around the vulnerable person (typically the young offender) whose interests you are there to protect. You should liase with the conference convenor and offer to help them in rallying a strong support group around a vulnerable offender. While there are troubled or "dysfunctional" families who are unable or unwilling to control the behaviour of the young person involved, it is important to keep in mind that any intervention by the state in the life of the young person involved will be unlikely to provide them with the kind of care and sense of belonging that they need in the long run. Long-term solutions are more likely to be found by creating and strengthening the social support network around vulnerable young people from their families, relations, neighbours, and friends. A restorative justice conference is one of the best ways to rally family support around a young person in trouble and at risk, and therefore you should make an effort to persuade as many people from their extended family to participate. If the young offender turns up with one or two members of their family who have little control over his or her behaviour, then taking the young person out of their family environment and institutionalising them may look like the only option. The picture can look very different, however, if a strong group of distant but caring supporters are present, as they will be likely to represent other, more promising alternatives.

Keeping young people in some kind of family environment should be strongly preferred over other, seemingly easier and more expedient alternatives. However, becoming further alienated from family as a result of leaving home is likely to become a source of further complications and difficulties. Even where the young person is at risk from their immediate family, institutionalising them is potentially short-sighted. It is much more preferable to bring along other relations who may offer to take the young person in, so that they are looked after by people who care about them as family.

If you have concerns about the safety of the young person within their family or the family's ability to care for them and control their behaviour, then you should definitely raise your concerns in the meeting or with trusted family members and the facilitator in confidence. This, however, must not lead to hidden agendas, collusion and manipulation behind the scene to fabricate an outcome against the express wishes of the people involved. The final decisions must lie with the young person and the wider family, whose presence and empowerment in the conference should be your priority.

10

FOR PROGRAM MANAGERS, REFERRING AGENTS AND POLICY MAKERS

Effective facilitation does not come about by accident. It must be developed through an infrastructure of support, training, case referrals, and feedback systems on practice quality. Without these, the potential of restorative justice programs cannot be realised. This is where program managers can and must make their mark. Without adequate support from program managers, practitioners will be unlikely to provide consistently good service. They will be struggling to deliver decent service, especially in unusual and high-risk cases, for sheer lack of skills.

Referring agencies are not less important. Without referrals from legal advocates, judges, magistrates, police, and corrections officers, well prepared conferencing programs can remain inactive or under utilised year after year, while ineffective and often counterproductive adversarial responses to criminal behaviour continue to be applied. The result is that important opportunities to make a positive difference in the lives of the people who suffer the worst consequences of crime continue to be lost. Like addictive behaviour, the system's approach only succeeds in generating more and more work for itself, because increased incarceration will only result in increased recidivism, which in turn leads to more incarceration, resulting in an impossible, vicious cycle that creates untold misery for so many people. The only winners are the professionals whose careers are built on servicing this insatiable, ever growing monster of criminal justice, while a horrendous price is being exacted from those caught up in it and the individuals and communities who pay for and ultimately suffer the consequences of criminal victimisation.

The quickest way to break this vicious cycle is through enlightened policy advice and legislation. Appropriate contributions from policy advisors and legislators are therefore crucial. Most individuals in agencies such as the courts, policing and corrections are unlikely to take risks in experimenting with something that is not sanctioned from above through appropriate laws and policy directives.

If you are a program manager

As a program manager, there are two main factors you should bear in mind for ensuring facilitator competence. First, there is the initial and ongoing training of facilitators. Second, ongoing feedback should be provided to facilitators.

Facilitator training

Successful facilitation requires sensitivity and skill. Good quality training for facilitators is now available from a variety of sources, including from this author. Budgetary constraints are understandable, but leaving people in conflict in the hands of facilitators who are untrained in appropriate conflict resolution and facilitation skills is irresponsible. An example of this is the New Zealand Youth Justice Conferencing Program. In over ten years of operation, conference convenors still haven't had competent training in conflict resolution and facilitation techniques. As a general rule, facilitators are thrown in at the deep end, and there is often a lack of continuity from one coordinator to the next. There is no policy in place about apprenticeship training, let alone properly designed conference facilitation training. From time-to-time there is a little tinkering around the edges in response to external pressure, but nothing substantial has changed.

Claims to the contrary are contradicted by high rates of re-offending, disempowerment and experiences of re-victimisation. Claims by apologists that early problems have been fixed have never been demonstrated and in this author's experience are not true, save the apparent policy change to keep potentially critical observers out of FGCs.

Feedback to facilitators

Simply collecting statistics on numbers of agreements and numbers of fulfilled agreements is not sufficient to indicate good practice and client satisfaction. A better way of measuring satisfaction is to have a brief questionnaire filled out anonymously by participants after each conference. The questionnaire should have appropriate categories to indicate the role of the respondent, such as offender, victim, friend, parent etc. It should be brief so as to ensure a high response rate. It needs to include qualitative questions concerning those things which in the opinion of the respondent were done well and those that should be improved.

Such feedback must be used for purposes of ongoing improvement in facilitation practice rather than punitively.

If you are a potential referring agent
Judge, magistrate, police, corrections officer etc

Ideally, restorative justice conferences should be used whenever the primary stakeholders are willing to meet to resolve their differences. Conferences can be used as an alternative to court, or as part of a court process, especially before sentencing in the more serious offence categories, as is done, for example, in the New Zealand Youth Court. They can also be used following sentencing to allow closure and healing to take place for those involved. Finally, they can be used privately in conflict situations that do not involve criminal proceedings.

Unfortunately, where community groups have set up conferencing programs, they tend to be under-utilised. Some programs have trained their facilitators but are not getting cases referred to them. As a judge, magistrate, police officer or correction officer, you often have discretion and influence over whether a case is referred to a restorative justice meeting. While advances have been made in the area of youth justice, progress is much slower in the area of adult offending. Many courts and police officers seem to regard the growing interest in, and need for, restorative interventions with indifference. Conferences appear to be viewed as irrelevant, unless, of course, appropriate legislation leaves the decision maker no choice but to make referrals. Even then, much is left to discretion, and whether referrals are made depends largely on the cooperation and good will of the relevant decision makers.

There is an obligation on you as a public servant to serve the public interest. This is your first and most important duty. Therefore, given the appearance of this promising new approach to crime interventions, it is your duty to examine its virtues and compare it to current practice in a dispassionate way, modifying practice as required by the public interest. The public interest in this instance largely coincides with the client's interest. If you are not sure about the effectiveness of this approach, then you at least have the duty to go along to some conferences and satisfy yourself as to the matter before deciding to ignore, or worse, oppose it.

If you see potential in what you observe but are not satisfied as to the quality of facilitation practice in your jurisdiction, try changing it or you may be able to become a facilitator yourself and run your own conferences under the aegis of your organisation, be it in policing, court, or corrections. What you need to ensure is that you have a good grasp of the principles of restorative justice and how they can be implemented. Basically, if you stick to the empowerment model and the facilitation instruments provided in the Appendices, you will not go wrong. These contain the accumulated wisdom and experience of many facilitators from a wide range of programs and contexts. It may take half a dozen or so conferences before you feel confident enough to handle the more difficult cases.

Conditions that make a referral appropriate are commonly that both parties are willing to meet and that liability or responsibility is admitted. In some jurisdictions, only the offender's consent and the admission of liability needs to be obtained for a conference to take place. The victim's consent is not required. When an offender such as a young person is at risk, a conference can be used as a way of enlisting the support of relevant people in the family and the community, and even if the victim does not attend, this can be a very important event in the offender's life, whereby problems are nipped in the bud before they deteriorate into serious wrongdoing.

Judges must be careful not to disempower the primary stakeholders by overruling their decisions when the case comes back to court, unless the agreement violates the law. If the judge has reservations, it may be better to refer the matter back to another conference, having stated the nature of the reservations.

Do not be satisfied with poor attendance at a conference. Insist that the conference be reconvened. For example, if no supporters of the offender attended the conference, that is hardly satisfactory. Especially if the case is serious or high risk, you should insist on a proper conference being run, with appropriate attendance by all interested parties, before approving and finalising the matter.

If you are a policy advisor or legislator

Bureaucrats in criminal justice institutions, police, the courts, and corrections, are often quite reluctant to refer cases for alternative, restorative justice processes, in spite of there being a clear need for better ways of administering justice.

The use of restorative justice conferences should be encouraged regardless of the degree of seriousness of the crime, or the age of the offender. This means that new legislation needs to be introduced, legislation that allows and requires criminal justice agencies, such as police, the courts, and corrections, to make available the option of restorative justice meetings between offenders and victims, and their respective families and communities of care and support. To date, this has been experimented with mostly in the area of juvenile crime, but, if anything, the need for introducing the restorative option is even greater in areas of adult crime, where the damage to people, and the need for effective interventions and healing seems all the more serious.

However, face-to-face meetings and discussions between the principal protagonists must be conducted by appropriately trained facilitators. Control and administration of such restorative justice programs should be placed in the hands of community groups, rather than centralised state bureaucracies, as this will maximise a program's flexibility to the socio-cultural and other environmental characteristics of the local community. The participation of the principal protagonists' respective communities (family members and trusted friends, colleagues, teachers, coaches, etc) is very important, especially in the more serious offence categories. It is the community of such supporters that is the best insurance that the voice of reason prevails in all matters and that stable and workable resolutions are reached.

Once again, the content and outcome of such facilitated meetings must not be determined by secondary stakeholders, such as the facilitator, social workers, legal advocates and the police, as that would disempower the principal parties in conflict and their satisfaction with justice would be significantly less likely. The full range of sanctions allowable by law must be made available to the community of participants in such restorative justice forums. Without this, their empowerment is incomplete and their ability to resolve the matter to everybody's satisfaction is limited. Indeed, given community values in terms of the appropriate and often necessary role of punitive measures in criminal justice responses to wrongdoing, especially where serious offences are concerned, communities of participants in restorative justice meetings must be empowered to apply the full range of sanctions allowed by law. The role of legal professionals, such as legal advocates and judges, in such cases should be to provide guidance to the participants in matters of law, so that decisions reached by the principal parties in such restorative justice meetings do not fall outside legal limits.

Criminal justice conflicts that prove irresolvable through restorative justice meetings can be dealt with through a modified court process where the victims of crime are empowered commensurately to their stake in seeing justice done in the court process. For criminal offences are, principally, wrongs done to specific people, the victims of the crime, not to the (dead) letter of the law, or even the (abstract entity of the) state. Therefore, the focus of the court process must be the victim and the wrong that was done to them. This should be reflected in a real transfer of the state's power to the victim, which implies major changes to the current court system.[1]

First, the victim must be given qualified legal representation by changing the role of the public prosecutor from being a representative of the state to being the victim's advocate. Second, the sentencing powers of judges must be shared with, and possibly transferred to, the victim. Third, offenders must be given the opportunity even in the sentencing stage to negotiate. The proper function of the legal professionals in such a modified court process is to ensure the smooth running of the conflict resolution process, ensuring that all parties act within the law, that everybody's rights and responsibilities are observed, that sentences are within limits set by law and that they do not obviously undermine the public good.

Since civil society has failed to protect victims from being wronged in the first instance, it is civil society's foremost obligation to ensure that they get every opportunity to satisfy themselves that justice is done. Most importantly, appropriate institutionalised frameworks, whereby victims' compliance with community values and the law are aided and monitored by communities of participants and legal experts, are sufficient to ensure that such victim empowerment does not result in an overstepping of the acceptable boundaries set by morality and law, resulting in an injustice to the offender. But once the requisite safeguards are in place, the rest is the prerogative of the victim, in negotiation with the offender. As with judges under the traditional court system, unless they clearly display unreasonable degrees of leniency or harshness, a victim's decision should be final.

Concluding remarks

The primary focus of criminal justice policy and reform must be the empowerment of the primary stakeholders in criminal justice conflicts. The primary stakeholders are the victim, the offender, and their respective communities of concern and care. These people are the ones most affected both by the criminal wrongdoing and by the way their case is subsequently handled and resolved by the system. It is they who have the most to lose or gain by the relevant criminal justice

---

1   See Barton 1999, Chapters 9 and 10, as well as the Afterword.

intervention. If it is done well, they free themselves from the burden of the past and move on. Conversely, if the intervention is done poorly, they will be trapped in a negative, self-destructive state, finding it hard to put the past behind them. Since it is these people who have the greatest interest in terms of knowing and feeling that justice has been done, their views, wishes, and priorities in terms of how their conflict should be resolved must take precedence over the views and priorities of third parties, such as legal professionals and other agents of the state.

While the state should ensure that there are both formal and informal processes of conflict resolution available for the resolution of criminal justice cases in culturally appropriate ways, professionals and agents of the state must not take over the parties' conflict. Their stake in justice is secondary and therefore their proper role is a supportive one and must be confined to the smooth running of the conflict resolution processes, ensuring that all parties act within the law, that everybody's rights and responsibilities are properly observed, and that agreements between the parties are not obviously harmful to the public interest.

Restorative justice meetings have the potential to repair the harm caused to individuals and communities through wrongdoing, conflict, and crime. However, restoration and healing do not happen automatically – they depend on good mediation and facilitation practice. Appropriate skills for each type of conflict resolution process must be acquired and developed by facilitators through competent training and ongoing quality monitoring and feedback systems. Seeking honest feedback from participants and observers enables facilitators to hone their skills and enjoy ongoing growth in understanding their work, other people, and themselves.

The importance of good practice cannot be emphasised enough. Apart from its obvious importance for the participants in face to face meetings, good practice is the best way to ensure that alternative conflict resolution processes will be widely adopted and used as a first choice of response to conflict, wrongdoing and crime and that traditional, adversarial processes will be used only as a fallback instrument of last resort.

Appendix 1:
SCRIPT FOR FACILITATORS

What to do before the conference (checklist)

1. Ensure that your facilitation instruments (main conference plan with scripted prompts, crisis management plans, the seating plan, as well as a pen and a notebook) are all ready for an immediate start, as soon as all participants have been seated.

2. Before the participants arrive, prepare the room, organise refreshments, and arrange the seating according to your seating plan.

3. Be ready to greet the participants upon arrival, and invite the parties to wait in separate areas.

4. When everyone is ready, invite the participants into the conference room and show them to their seats. Seat the observers and secondary stakeholders first, victim party next, offender party last, especially if the conference is large.

To everybody:

> I have prepared a seating plan. Please take your seats as indicated, so that I can tell who is sitting where.

5. As soon as people have been seated, *start*:

Introduction and preliminaries

To everybody:

1. Welcome everybody. Before the formal part of the conference begins, I would like us to introduce ourselves and indicate briefly our reasons for being here. I am [*name_____*] and I will be facilitating today's conference.

A template for seating plans

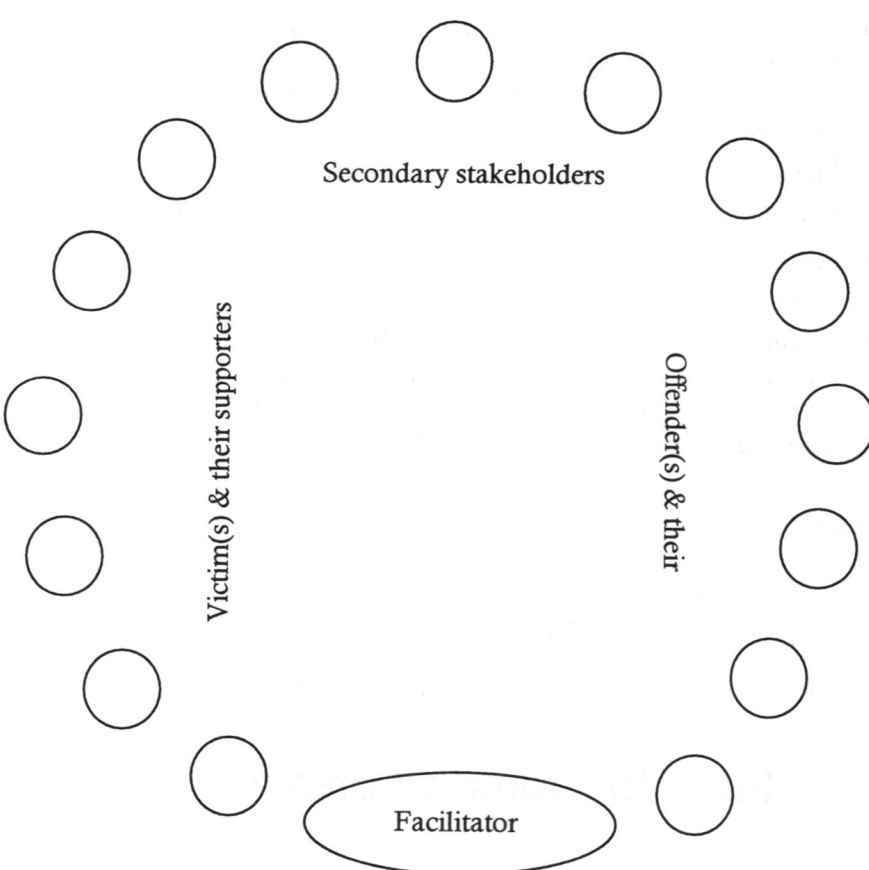

Secondary stakeholders

Victim(s) & their supporters

Offender(s) & their

Facilitator

Go around the circle, gesturing towards each participant. While they are introducing themselves, double check your seating plan.

2. Thank you everybody, and thank you all for making the effort to attend. Today's conference will focus on the [*brief description, eg, stone throwing, etc ...*] incident, which happened [_ _ _ _ _ _ _ _] days or weeks ago. First, we will focus on what [*first name(s) of offender(s)* _ _ _ _ _ _ _ _ _ _ _ _ _ _ _ _ _ _] did, and how their behaviour has affected others. After this there will be an opportunity for all of you to consider possible ways of repairing the harm that has resulted and express your views as to what you would like to see happen from here.

    I must emphasise at this point that there is absolutely no expectation of you as an individual, or as a group, that you will come to any particular agreement. Indeed, it is important that you all feel free to agree or disagree with any particular view or proposal, and that you do not agree to anything that is not right for you. This case does not have to be resolved here, and you should not agree to anything that does not seem right to you. Does everybody understand this?

Look around the room to check if people understand and agree with these proposals.

To the offender(s):

3. [*First name(s) of offender(s)* _ _ _ _ _ _ _ _ _ _ _ _ _ _ _ _], you have admitted your part in this incident. All the same, if at any stage in this conference you do not wish to continue, you are free to leave. If you choose to leave, this matter will not be finalised here, and may be dealt with differently. The matter can be finalised by this meeting, provided that consensus is reached, and that you fulfil any agreements that may be jointly decided. It is important, therefore, that you take an active role in discussions and decisions.

If conditions are different, such as when no formal agreement is required, or when the agreement has to be presented to a sentencing judge for their approval, they should be stated as appropriate.

To everybody:

4. I would like to remind everybody that the matters you will be discussing here require sensitivity and confidentiality, and that the privacy of all participants must be protected through anonymity.

5. In terms of the process, I will ask each of you to speak one at a time and contribute your views and thoughts on the matter. It is important that everybody is allowed to speak without interruption. If at any stage any of you would like to have a break to discuss your concerns in private, please do not hesitate to indicate. Before any agreements are finalised, I will give everybody a chance for a private session so that any concerns you may have can be discussed in the privacy of your group. It will then be up to you to raise those matters for consideration when we reconvene.

6. Is all of that clear to everybody? Does anybody have any questions about the process at this point?

Look around the room, and give a chance for people to respond.

7. If you have any questions at any stage, please do not hesitate to ask.

Stage I: Exploration

Step 1. To the offender(s)

Prompt each one in turn:

1. [*First name(s) of offender(s)*_____],
    before you tell this meeting about what happened and the way you got involved, is there anything you want to say?

2. Tell us what happened. How did you get involved? Then, what happened?

3. What was going through your mind at the time? What were you hoping to achieve?

4. How did you feel about what you did *immediately afterwards?*

5. What do you think *now* of what you did?

6. Have there been any changes in your life since this incident? What were they? Any other changes?

7. Who has been affected by this? How do you think they were affected? Who else has been affected? How do you think they were affected?

If the offender forgets to mention people who have been significantly affected, such as the victim, their own family, their school or colleagues, and finally themselves, ask the offender:

8. How do you think [_____] has been affected? And, how do you feel about that?

9. How has this affected you?

Now is the time for the offender and/or other participants to clarify and acknowledge responsibility. This should include explicitly clearing the victim of blame.

10. Who do you think is responsible for this incident?

11. Do you blame [*the victim* _____] for any of this? Do you blame anybody else?

A. If NOT BLAMING, skip to prompt 13.
B. If BLAMING, continue:

12. Would you explain why?

C. If still BLAMING, skip immediately to your Crisis Management Plan *(included in Appendix 2, p 157).*

Especially if the victim is being blamed, there is a potential crisis on your hands. The victim is in danger of being re-victimised. Your *Crisis Management Plan* is designed to reduce that risk and diffuse the crisis.

13. Finally, is there anything else you would like to add or say at this point?

When finished:

Thank you.

Step 2. To the offender supporters

Prompt each in turn:

1. How did you find out initially about what happened?

2. What did you think when you first heard?

3. What has happened since?

4. How do you feel about the incident now? What are the main issues for you?

5. And where are you inclined to place responsibility for what happened?

6. Do you blame [*the victim_____*] for any of this?

A. If NO, skip to prompt 8.
B. If YES, ask:

7. Would you please explain what exactly you blame them for, and why?

If necessary, use the appropriate sections of *Crisis Management Plan*, as outlined further below (see Appendix 2).

8. Is there anything else you want to add?

Step 3. To the primary victim(s)

Prompt each one in turn:

1. Thank you for being patient. Please tell us about the way you experienced this incident, and what it has meant for *you?*

Additional prompts:

2. Tell us what happened. What were you doing at the time? Then, what happened?

3. What thoughts were racing through your mind when all this was going on?

4. How did your family and friends react when they first heard? How are they feeling about it now?

5. How has this affected you? And, how do you feel about that?

6. What has been happening for you since the incident?

7. Has this affected anybody else who is not here today? How were they affected? Anybody else who has been affected? Anybody else?

For every person who has been significantly affected and is absent from the meeting, but whom the victim forgets to mention (such as their family members and friends, the school or their colleagues, etc) prompt:

8. Has this affected [*so and so_____*]?
    How were they affected?
    How about [*so and so_____*]?
    Have they been affected? How were they affected?

9. Have you been inclined to blame yourself for any of this?

A. If NO, skip to prompt 12.
B. If YES, continue:

10. Would you explain why?

Then, ask the whole group:

>   11. Would anybody like to comment on that?

>   12. Finally, is there anything else you would like to add or say, or any questions you might want to ask [*the offender*_____], or anybody else at this point?

When finished:

>   Thank you.

Step 4. To the victim supporters

Prompt each one in turn:

>   1.   [*Name of person*_____], What did you think when you first heard?

>   2.   What has happened since?

>   3.   How do you feel about what happened?

>   4.   How has this affected [*the victim*_____]?

>   5.   And how has it affected you?

>   6.   What are the main issues for you?

>   7.   Finally, is there anything else you would like to add or say, or any questions you would like to ask [*the offender*_____], or anybody else at this point?

When finished:

>   Thank you.

Step 5. To the secondary stakeholders

Prompt each one in turn:

1. What are your thoughts on this matter?
   Is there anything you would like to raise at this point?
   What are the main issues for you?

2. How has this affected you personally?
   (and/or) How are people generally affected in these kinds of cases?
   What tend to be the consequences?
   Would you be able to give an example?
   How did that affect you?

When finished:

   Thank you.

Step 6. The hardest thing for everybody

Prompt each participant one-by-one:

   What has been the hardest thing for you in this? or What did you find the most difficult about this incident?

Stage II: Transition – Opportunity for symbolic reparation

Step 7. To the offender

   [*Offender's name*_____], it may not have been easy for you to sit through and listen to what everyone has had to say. You have heard people describe the way they were affected by what you did. Before moving on to consider how this matter might be resolved, is there anything you want to say to them?

A. If NO, skip to Step 9: Offender Supporters.
B. If YES, continue:

143

Step 8. To the victim

Is there anything you would like to say in response?

Step 9. To the offender supporters

Is there anything you want to say to
[*the victim*_____] or
[*the offender*_____] , or anybody else,
before we move on?

Step 10. To the victim (and others who might have been spoken to at Step 3)

Is there anything you would like to say (in response or
to anybody here) before we move on?

Step 11. Determine whether the meeting will continue

At this point it may be useful to confirm with everybody that they wish to proceed to the agreement stage. In cases where an agreement is not appropriate, the conference should be closed at this point, using the appropriate prompts. Therefore choose between *A* and *B*:

A. If an agreement is not applicable, skip to Closing the Conference (p 154).
B. If an agreement is applicable, continue:

To everybody:

Thank you everybody. Now that you have considered
in detail what happened and the way people were
affected, I would like to know where you want to go
from here. Do you wish to continue this meeting to see
if you can come to an agreement about the future? The
alternative would be to reconvene and continue
another time, or simply finish here. As I said at the

> beginning, there is no expectation that you arrive at
> any particular outcome in this meeting. With that in
> mind, what would you like to do?

Look around and, if the reaction is not obvious or unanimous, prompt
people for their responses.

A. If CONTINUING, go to Stage III: Agreement on p 145.
B. If NOT CONTINUING, proceed:

Step 12. To those who do not want to continue

1. The case needs to be resolved one way or another.
    Would you like to continue another time instead?
    How would you like to see the case being finalised?
    Any suggestions? Any other suggestions?

2. What do others think of that?
    What do you think of it [*name_____*]?
    What about you [*name_____*]?

Encourage and allow discussion by the group. If applicable, arrange the
date and time for reconvening, then close the meeting. Close the
conference using the appropriate prompts – skip to *Closing the Conference*
on p 154.

If people decide to continue, got to the next step.

Stage III: Agreement

Step 13. To offender and supporters

Ask each, starting with the offender:

1. [*Name of offender/offender supporters, prompted
    one-by-one_____*], Do you think that
    something further should be done to put things right?
    Why/ why not?

A. If NO, go to the next person, repeating the same prompts.
B. If YES, continue:

> 2. What have you thought of?
>   Do you have any suggestions?
>   Any other suggestions?

Make a note of every suggestion, so that you may check them all later with the group, then go to the next person in the offender's support group.

Step 14. Victim and supporters

Ask each, starting with the victim:

> 1. [*Name of victim/victim supporters,*_____]
>   What would *you* like to see come out of this conference?
>   What would *you* consider to be a fair agreement?
>
> 2. Any (other) suggestions?

Make a note of every suggestion, so that you may check them all later with the group.

Step 15. To everybody else remaining, such as third parties and professionals, one-by-one

> 1. [*Name of person, one-by-one*_____]
>   What would *you* like to see happen? What would *you* consider to be a desirable and fair agreement?
>
> 2. Any (other) suggestions?

Make a note of every suggestion, so that you may check them all later with the group.

Step 16. To the offender, followed by the group, as appropriate

> 1. [*Name of offender(s)*_____] You have heard people's suggestions for an agreement. What do you think of what has been suggested so far?
>   What would *you* like to do to put things right?

146

Next, cover the offender(s) suggestions one-by-one, followed by the rest of the suggestions on your list that were made earlier:

2. **What do others think of [proposal 1, 2, 3 ... etc]?**

Check each proposal one-by-one with the victim and their supporters and with the offender's supporters, then with everyone else, prompting them by name if necessary, one-by-one:

3. [*So and so* _____] **What do you think of that?**

Ensure that all suggestions are considered. Additional prompts for facilitating the ensuing discussion are:

4. **What do others think of that? [***Name of person,***
   especially the other party_____] **How
   does that sit with you? What are your thoughts?
   Does that seem like a fair suggestion?
   If not, why not?
   Is that practicable/feasible?
   How do you feel about that?**

Step 17. Checking all points of agreement and disagreement with all participants (especially those who have not been involved so far in discussing the agreement)

1. **What do you think of the proposals so far?
   Are they appropriate?
   Are they fair?
   Are they as good as they can be in the circumstances?
   Why?/Why not?**

2. **Are all these proposals together too much or not enough?
   Why?/Why not?**

3. **Do you have any other suggestions?
   Anything else that should be considered?
   What do others think of that suggestion?
   Would that be appropriate?
   Would that be fair?
   Would it improve the agreement?
   Why?/Why not?**

Step 18. Private session

This can be optional, but the presumption should be strongly in favour of having it, especially if you have doubts about the proposed agreement, or the parties' satisfaction with it. Do not skip private sessions lightly, but request them as a matter of routine. There must be three conditions met by the meeting to justify not having a private session:

a. There must be no tension or reticence shown by any of the participants by this stage of the conference

b. All present must clearly and convincingly indicate that they do not wish to have a private session.

c. You must be comfortable with the way the conference has progressed.

If any of these conditions is not fulfilled, or you have doubts, ask to see the parties in private. More often than not, you will be surprised by what comes out in the privacy of each group.

1. At this point, and before any agreements are finalised, I would like to give you all the opportunity to have a private session with your own group. Private sessions are confidential, and they allow you to raise and discuss amongst yourselves any concerns you may have about the way the conference has been going and the proposed agreement. Points of concern may then be raised for further discussion when we reconvene.

Proceed with *A. Requesting a Private Session* or *B. Offering a Private Session* as appropriate at this point.

A. Requesting a private session

Indicate your wish to have a quick session with *both* parties, even if you really need to check things out with only one of them. This is important for maintaining your neutrality before the parties.

> May I please see each group in turn for a brief private session? I assure you all of my confidentiality and commitment to remain neutral. It will be your decision whether to raise for discussion any issues we touch on during the private session when we reconvene.
> (Choose to see the party that seems to be at unease the most.) May I see Party A/B first, please? In the meantime, the rest of you can take a break.

Skip to *Step 19 Facilitating the Private Session* on p 149.

B. *Offering a private session*

When a private session seems unnecessary, check with the meeting:

> How do people feel about having a short break for a
> private session? Would anybody like to have a break?
> [*So and so*_____] would you like to
> have a break before we continue?

If people want to continue without a break, go to *Step 21 Finalising
the Agreement* (p 153). If, however, there is no consensus, or you sense
the need to check things with some of the participants, return to
A. Requesting a Private Session.

Step 19. Facilitating the private session

1. This is a private session and it gives you an opportunity
   to identify issues and concerns that may not have been
   adequately addressed up to this point. As such,
   everything discussed here is confidential. It will be up
   to you whether you want to raise any points discussed
   with the other party.

Ask the following questions:

2. How is the conference going for you?

3. Do you have any concerns?

4. Is there anything else relevant that has not been raised,
   or inadequately considered?

5. Is the proposed agreement fair? Is it realistic? If not,
   why not? Are there better alternatives?

Cover briefly each point of the proposed agreement, as well as points of
disagreement one-by-one:

6. What do you think of the proposal to [_____]?

7. Do you want anything changed? If so, in what way,
   and why? Would that make for a better agreement?
   What if the other party still does not think so?

8. Which of these points should be raised when we reconvene? Who will raise them?

9. What would you like to see happen if you do not reach agreement here? What do you think is likely to happen? Would that still be better for you than what the other party suggested?

At end of session:

10. Finally, I wish to assure you once again that everything discussed here is confidential: I am not going to tell the other party of these discussions. I will give you the opportunity, however, to raise any new points with them when we reconvene.

Step 20. Post-caucus negotiations and agreement

If there was a private session, prompt both sides, as groups and as individuals:

1. Are there any issues or new points arising from your discussions that you would like to raise for consideration?

2. [Name_____] are there any points you would like to raise?

Then, ask other participants, individually and/or collectively, to respond to any points raised.

3. What do others think of that? Would anybody like to comment?

4. [Name of person_____], what do *you* think?

5. Should the proposed agreement be changed to take it into account?

6. What do you propose? What do others think of that?

7. Any other points that anybody else would like to see
    discussed or considered? And, what do others think of
    that? Anything else?

Allow people to discuss any changes that they would like to see made,
and then continue with the prompts below.

Step 21. Finalising the agreement or disagreement

Choose between *A* or *B*.
Skip to *B* if there is no agreement between participants (p 152).

A. If An Agreement Has Been Formed
To everybody:

1. Is there anything else you can think of as being relevant
    to putting this matter to rest? Is there anything that has
    not been heard, or anything that has been mentioned
    but not adequately considered so far?

Prompt people by name individually: first the victim, then the victim
supporters, then the offender, then the offender supporters, and finally
the rest of the conference.

2. Anything else that should be taken into account?
    Any other important matters that you/anybody
    can think of?

3. If there are no further matters to be discussed, I
    would like to summarise the main points of the
    proposed agreement and check that everybody is
    happy with them.

Summarise the agreement in point format, and then check with the
participants, and with the offender and their supporters in particular:

4. Is this agreement fair?
    Is it realistic?
    If not, why not?

5. Are you aware of any difficulties that are likely to
    interfere with the agreement being completed?
    Any other difficulties you can think of?

6. Should anything be changed in the agreement?

If YES:

> Would that be more appropriate?
> Would it still be fair?
> Would that make for a better agreement?
> What do others think of the proposed changes?
> Anybody else?
> Anything else?

7. Any other changes?

8. If there are no further changes, I will write up the agreement and have it signed before you leave so that you can take a copy with you.

Skip to *Step 22: Finalising the Arrangements.*

B. If An Agreement Has Not Taken Shape

9. I would like to reassure everybody that there is no expectation that you reach agreement in this meeting. Keeping that in mind, I can summarise and put into writing the various points on which you agree and disagree, indicating your respective views on each point. Alternatively, you can give it one more try before we bring the meeting to a close. What would you like to do?

Prompt each participant by calling out their names and asking:

10. [*Name_____*] What would you like to do?

When finished:

> Thank you.

A. If NOT CONTINUING, skip back to **Step 12 To those who do not want to continue** *(p 145).*
B. If CONTINUING, restart from **Stage III: Agreement** *and follow the prompts as you see appropriate.*

Step 22. Finalising the arrangements

1. Before closing the conference, I would like one or two volunteers to be my contacts, people who will support [*the offender*_____] in honouring what has been decided here today, and who will also monitor progress of the agreement. Who would like to help with that? Anybody else who would like to help?

2. Thank you. And what would be the best way to contact you? And could you please let me know immediately if there are any difficulties with meeting the deadline?

3. Finally, I must check with you all what you would like to see happen in the event that the agreement is not fulfilled. One option could be to reconvene the conference to discuss the matter with [*the offender*_____] and make a decision from there. Or you may want to suggest something else. What do people think?

Look around the room to check with people what they would like to see done, and allow them to discuss and reach consensus.

4. And what about reconvening if the agreement is completed?
   How do people feel about that?

If the consensus is to reconvene:

5. Shall we put down a date for it?

6. Are there any other issues that need to be clarified or followed up?

6. Is everybody clear about what they are supposed to do, whom they need to contact, and by when? Do you need to exchange numbers now, or make arrangements?

Allow people to exchange contact details and make arrangements.

Closing the conference

1. Prior to closing the conference,

2. is there anything else anyone wants to say? Anything else?

2. In closing, I would like to thank you all for coming and contributing to the meeting.

Unless already covered, indicate any actions to be taken by you or others, for example:

3. We will reconvene at [*date, place, time of follow-up conference*_ _ _ _ _ _ _ _ _ _ _ _ _ _ _ _ _ _].

4. If there is anything further I can be of help to you, please do not hesitate to contact me. I wish you all well, and invite you to stay for refreshments. I hope you can join us. Once again, many thanks.

While refreshments are being served, write up the agreement and have it signed by the principal parties and supporters. If possible, give them a copy each before they leave. Alternatively, send them a copy as soon as possible.

END

What to do after the conference (checklist)

1. Ensure that the principal parties have a copy of the agreement.

2. Contact the key participants within 1-3 days to check how they are faring, the way they feel about the meeting, and whether they need any assistance.

3. Monitor fulfilment of agreement and keep relevant stakeholders informed about progress.

4. Inform conference participants of final disposition of the case, especially the victim.

Appendix 2:
CRISIS MANAGEMENT PLAN

Averting re-victimisation

The following plan is developed to illustrate a way in which defiance or denial of responsibility by the offender and their supporters can be handled in a way that safeguards the victim. However, the same kind of procedure can be adopted and used with appropriated modifications to address all kinds of problems, including those caused by a very upset victim who may not be able to move on and let go of their anger. The idea of studying this plan by facilitators is not necessarily that it should be followed to the letter, but that the approach may be understood and then applied flexibly to meet the needs of particular situations.

The guiding principle behind managing crises is to face and confront the matter causing the crisis by first identifying and clarifying it, and then prompting the participants to discuss and express their views and feelings about what has been said. The opposite strategy, of suppressing conflict and ignoring provocative comments is ultimately self-defeating because it has a strong likelihood of leaving the affected people feeling disempowered and unhappy and sometimes more angry and resentful than they were before. Alternative conflict resolution works by bringing conflicts and disagreements into the open so that they can be collectively considered and resolved.

This Crisis Management Plan is a good example of how a potentially explosive situation can be faced and handled with calm and confidence by using that principle.

Step 23. Clarification of responsibility

To the offender, or the person(s) who is doing the blaming:

1. What exactly are you blaming [*the victim,
   or whoever else_ _ _ _ _ _ _ _ _ _ _ _ _ _ _ _ _*] for?
   In what way do you think they were responsible?

2. Does that excuse what [*you/the offender_ _ _ _ _ _ _ _ _ _ _*]
   has done?

Why?/Why not?
Would you mind explaining that please?

3. What is your view of [*your/the offender(s)* _ _ _ _ _ _ _ _ _]
    part in the incident?

Then you should immediately turn to the other offender supporters.

To the offender supporters, ask each of them:

4. Do you agree with that? or What is your view of
   blaming [*the victim/so and so* _ _ _ _ _ _ _ _ _ _ _ _ _ _ _ _ _] in
   the way suggested?

If unclear:

5. Would you explain that? or What do you mean?

A. If victim no longer blamed

If, having asked the same questions of all the offender supporters, you find that there is consensus amongst them that the victim is not to be blamed, continue to explore their views about the incident and its consequences by returning to where you left off in the main Conference Plan.

B. If victim still blamed

Whenever you find that someone is inclined to allocate blame to the victim, your questioning of that person must be more thorough before moving on to the next person. This means asking additional questions:

5. And, what is your view of [*the offender's* _ _ _ _ _ _ _ _ _ _]
    part in the incident?

6. Does what [*the victim* _ _ _ _ _ _ _ _ _ _ _ _ _ _ _ _] did
    excuse what [*the offender* _ _ _ _ _ _ _ _ _ _ _ _ _ _ _ _ _]
    has done?
    Why? Why not?

A. If victim no longer blamed

Chances are that offender supporters, and indeed the offender themselves, will be of the view that the victim's behaviour, or whatever the victim might have done, does not excuse the offender's behaviour, in which case you should resume where you left off in the main conference plan.

B. If victim still blamed

If the answers from offender supporters suggest that the offender's behaviour is excusable because of something the victim had done, then probably this conference should not have been convened in the first place. Do not terminate the conference, however, but first ask the victim, then their supporters, and finally all the secondary stake holders for their views on what has been said.

Step 24. The victim's perspective on responsibility

To the victim, then to victim supporters, and secondary stakeholders:

1. [*Name*_____], thank you for being patient. Do you agree with that? What is your view of all that has been discussed?

2. Does what [*you, the victim*_____] did excuse what [*the offender*_____] has done?

3. Why?/Why not?
   What should [*the offender and/or you, the victim*_____] have done, instead?

Step 25. Secondary stakeholder's perspective on responsibility

To the secondary stakeholders:

1. Thank you for being patient. Do you agree with that? What is your view of all that has been discussed?

2. Does what [*the victim*_____] did
   excuse what [*the offender*_____] has
   done?

3. Why?/Why not? What should [*the offender and/or the*
   *victim*_____] have done, instead?

A. If consensus is reached

Allow participants to discuss among themselves the various degrees of responsibility that are appropriate for each party. In some cases, victims will acknowledge that they could have handled the situation differently, themselves. Cases are not always black and white, and this possibility must always be allowed for in the process. The crucial question that must be clarified in the course of such discussions is whether, and to what extent, the offender's behaviour is excusable on account of what the victim, or someone else had done. As soon as questions of responsibility are sorted out, resume the normal course of the conference where you left off.

B. If consensus is not reached

If, after a period, consensus seems unlikely and relations worsen, then you should raise the possibility of terminating the conference with the participants, but not without you having a private session with them first, which will also give both sides a chance to have time out in a private session by themselves, while you are talking with the other party.

Step 26. Private session/caucus

To everybody:

1. At this point, I would like to see each group in private to check and explore with you separately the possible options that may be open to you from here, including the option of terminating the conference, if that is what you decide to do. I want to assure you all that I will continue to remain neutral in all matters, and that all decisions will be yours. Private sessions are confidential, and it will be up to you to raise any issues discussed when we reconvene.

Choose to see the party that is the most upset first.

2. Can I see Party A/B first? In the meantime the rest of you may take a break.

In the private session, use the following prompts with both groups:

3. What are your concerns?

4. What do you think are the main issues for the other party? Are these valid? How would you handle the matter if you were in their place? What do you think of that? [Name_____] do you agree? Why/Why not?

5. Is there anything else relevant that has not been raised so far?

6. Should these be raised when the conference reconvenes? If so, how and who will raise them?

7. How do you feel about terminating the conference?

8. What would be the likely result if such was decided?

9. Would that be preferable to continuing with it?

Note: Even if a group wishes to terminate the conference, encourage them to reconvene and explain to the other party why they wanted to do that. This will give the other party a chance to appreciate their point of view and respond. In some cases they may then agree jointly to terminate the discussion, but their exchange may also start a new round of discussions, which can result in a successful agreement.

Following your private session with both groups, reconvene the conference and ask the parties whether there is anything that they would like to say.

Step 27: Post-caucus clarification

A. Upon reconvening, start with the offender:

1. [Name_____], has there been any change in the way you view the earlier discussed issues? How do you see things now?

2. Is there anything else you would like to bring up?

B. *To offender supporters, ask each in turn:*

1. What is your view?
   Do you agree with that? Why?/Why not?

2. Any other issues that need to be raised?

C. *To the victim, and each victim supporter in turn:*

1. What is your view? Is there anything (else) you would like to say?

D. *To all secondary stakeholders, ask each one:*

1. How do you see things? Do you have any suggestions? Do you have anything (else) you would like to say?

Step 28. Decision whether to continue or terminate the meeting

Choose between *A* and *B* as appropriate.

A. *If a consensus appears to have emerged about responsibility (or whatever else caused the crisis):*

1. May I check with you all whether you are ready to continue this meeting?

Prompt everybody in turn.

2. [*So and so_____*] what do you think?
   What would you like to do?

3. And what do others think of that?
   Anybody else?
   Any other suggestions?

If interactions have not improved, but worsened, summarise clearly the principal reasons for the disagreement and check with the parties what they want to do. More specifically, check with them whether they are happy to agree to disagree on those points and still continue the conference, or whether they wish to finish the discussion. If this is the choice of either party, explain to the participants the likely steps that will be taken from here, and thank them all for their time and participation. To do this, got to *Step 21 (B) If Agreement Has Not Taken Shape* in the main script and follow the prompts.

B. If a consensus has not emerged

1. The case needs to be resolved one way or another. Would you like to continue another time instead? How would you like to see the case being finalised? Any suggestions? Any other suggestions?

2. What do others think of that?
   What do you think of it [*name_____*]?
   What about you [*name_____*]?

Encourage and allow discussion by the group. If applicable, arrange the date and time for reconvening, then close the meeting. Close the conference using the appropriate prompts – skip to *Closing the Conference* on p 154.

If people decide to continue, got to the next step.

If the parties are happy to continue, return to where you left off in the main plan.

END

Appendix 3:
ROLE PLAYS

Role plays are a powerful and safe way to teach and learn conflict resolution skills. This is especially true in restorative justice, where serious criminal matters often represent vastly heightened stakes for the parties. As much as possible, the development of facilitator competence must not be at their expense, but must be developed, polished and maintained through realistic and well-designed role plays where tensions and conflict are built into the roles for the benefit of both practising and trainee facilitators.

The hints and suggestions below are based on my experience in running role plays with various groups in Australia, New Zealand and the United States. These are followed by two sample role plays.

For training purposes you can obtain the fully developed and prepared versions of these and other role plays, complete with tailored facilitation prompts based on the Empowerment Model of group conference facilitation. They are available online from the publisher at <www.federationpress.com.au>.

Hints and suggestions
for running role plays

1. Read Chapter 5 in this book on preparing and running face-to-face restorative justice meetings and prepare and run your role play as if it was the real thing. If you take it seriously, the role-players will do the same. You are doing yourself and the people in your charge a disservice if you start facilitating face-to-face meetings before you are able to facilitate realistic role plays smoothly and efficiently.

2. When allocating roles in a group, try to avoid allocating female roles to male participants. In my experience, most men have difficulties identifying with a female role, and in response to being called a "Mrs Smith," often end up acting silly. Women don't seem to have corresponding difficulties with male roles.

3. Before starting, provide each role player with a separate, individualised sheet of paper with the following information on it:

    a) Some basic instructions about how best the roles can be played. Some people have never experienced a role play, and unless alerted otherwise, they may innocently blurt out their entire roles at first chance, instead of waiting to be prompted for relevant contributions at appropriate times.

b) A general description of the incident captured in the role play.

c) Individual role description (but never the role description of any other players), indicating who they are, what their experience has been, their emotions, fears, hopes and expectations with regard to the incident and its resolution.

d) A brief list of names, telling them who the (other) characters are in the face-to-face meeting. The names of the "participants" should be listed in order of seating; say from left to right, relative to the facilitator. Without this, role players tend to become confused as to who is who in the meeting, and can find it difficult and awkward to address each other as a consequence.

(Fully tailored pages for role plays are available online from the publisher. See details above.)

4. Before starting, allow the participants to read through the information sheet provided and their respective roles, and check with them that everything is clear to them. Confused role players cannot get into their roles properly and can create unnecessary distractions. If anyone has general questions, answer them in the group. However, if a role player asks about how they should interpret and play their particular role, then it is best if you talk to them quietly, so that the inbuilt tensions and conflicts are not prematurely elicited to the other players. Each role player should start out ignorant of what other people are about in "the meeting". This will help in realistically simulating the inherent lack of certainty in conflict situations for both the facilitator and the participants. With particularly complex roles, it is a good idea to pull the role player aside and give them some hints about some of the more demanding episodes they are supposed to play out, such as an outburst of emotion, a spontaneous threat and expression of anger. The aim is to create realistic tensions and emotions through conflicts that are built into the roles, so that the facilitator can practise and hone their skills.

5. Make it a habit of not expecting consensus being reached by the parties, not even in role plays. The worst fallacy in conflict resolution is the definition of facilitator success and failure in terms of what the parties in conflict may and may not decide to do. Instead,

define your success in terms of having empowered all parties individually and collectively to discuss and resolve matters in any way that is right for them within the law. Keep reminding yourself that they are free agents and disagreement is their prerogative. You must always be prepared to close a meeting without agreement having been reached.

6. After conclusion of a role play, you must immediately "de-role" and debrief each participant. Some role players can get stuck in their role and remain disturbed and upset by it. For some role players, the role brings back painful memories. You must, therefore, make it a habit of "de-roling" each role player. This can be done in three to four easy steps. While the participants are still seated, go around the circle and ask them in turn:

   a) their real name;

   b) one thing which is different about them in real life from the role they just played;

   c) the most important insight they might have gained through playing that particular role (allow only a very short amount of time for this, so that everyone can be de-roled before more in-depth discussions);

   d) thank the person for their participation and take back the role description page you have given them at the beginning (unless you are happy for them to keep it).

7. After de-roling the participants, allow at least 30 minutes of discussion time about the role play and ask participants to give you honest feedback on what you did well, and where you might be able to further improve. (A lot of learning – not just for you, but for everybody – occurs at this time, while experiences, ideas and insights are shared in the group.)

8. Finally, enjoy your role plays. They are a fun and safe way to grow in confidence while learning new skills and about yourself and your reactions under stress.

Broken windscreen: A role play

Courtesy of Margaret Thorsborne and the
Restorative Justice Group, NSW Police Service
Edited by Charles Barton at Charles Sturt University

FACILITATOR'S MASTER GUIDE

The incident – case description

Three ninth grade boys wagging lessons after morning tea ended up on a pedestrian overpass near the school. They began throwing stones onto traffic passing underneath, eventually breaking a windscreen. The car stopped and the boys fled to the bushes on the side of the road. The owner of the car caught one of the boys, "manhandled" him into the car and drove him to the local police station. The police brought him back to school where the other two boys, seeing the police car arrive, reported themselves to the Principal. The three boys were suspended. The boys' families made overtures to the owner of the car to pay for the new windscreen. This incident occurred not long after a similar situation in another State had caused the death of a motorist.

Instruction to participants

This is an educational role play. Please keep fairly close to your assigned role, and try playing it realistically, especially when it comes to filling in the gaps in the script. Do not read out your role all in one go. The facilitator will prompt you for the relevant information at appropriate times. If you feel that your particular role, or the role play as a whole, is not realistic, you should raise your concerns in discussion afterwards. Disruption of the role-play diminishes its educational impact.

De-roling and debriefing

Immediately after the role play, and while participants are still seated, go around the circle and ask each person:

*   their real name
*   one thing which is different about them from the role they played
*   any insights they might have gained from playing that role

Broken windscreen seating plan

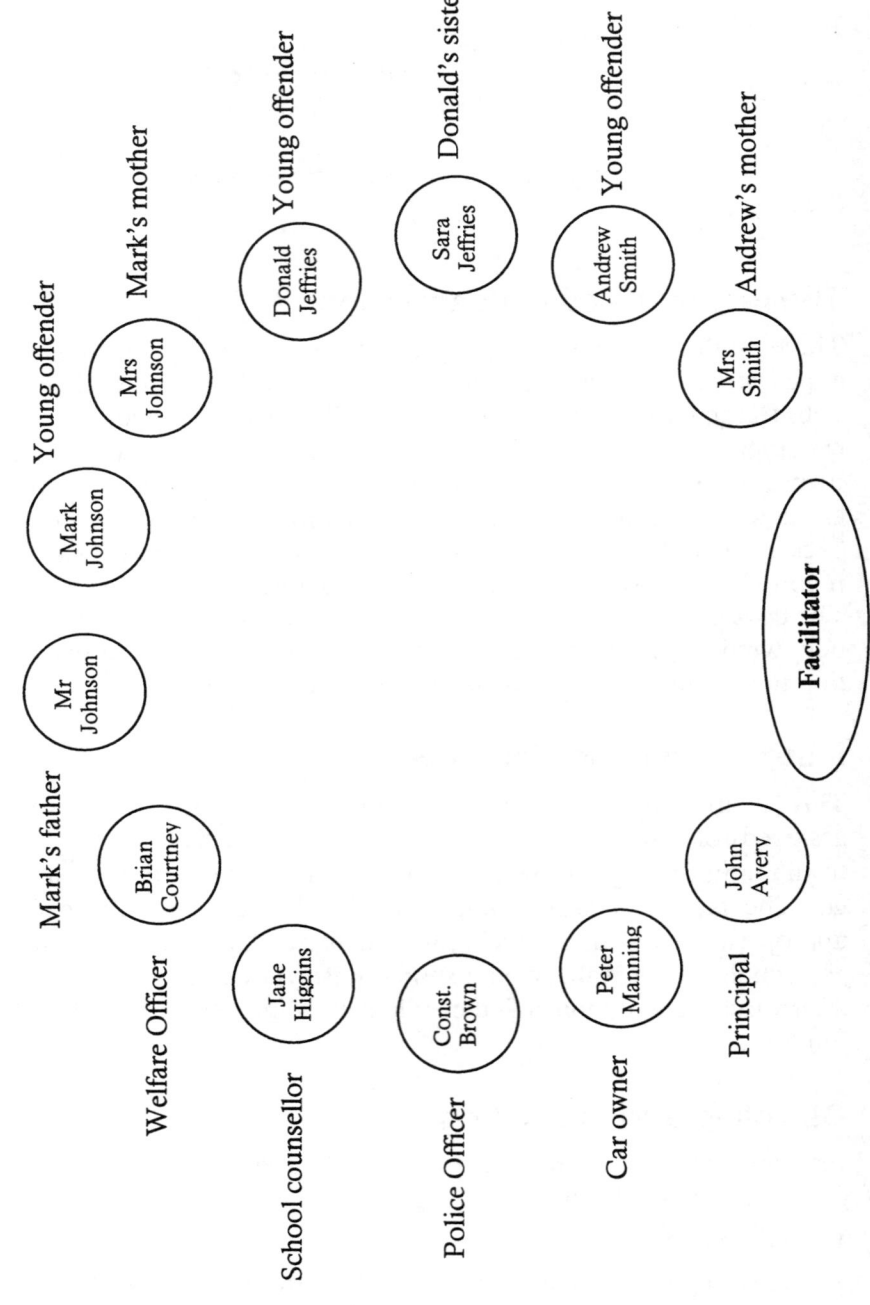

Young offender — Mark's mother

Young offender — Donald's sister

Young offender — Andrew's mother

Mrs Johnson

Donald Jeffries

Sara Jeffries

Andrew Smith

Mark Johnson

Mrs Smith

Mr Johnson

Facilitator

Mark's father — Brian Courtney

Welfare Officer — Jane Higgins

School counsellor — Const. Brown

Police Officer

Car owner — Peter Manning

John Avery

Principal

ROLE DESCRIPTIONS FOR PARTICIPANTS

JOHN AVERY (Principal)

You were pulled out of a meeting by the arrival of the police with Andrew. You were told by the ninth grade year coordinator that Andrew had been assaulted and kidnapped by a passing motorist. Then the two boys arrived in your office!

You felt disappointed, shocked and angry (although you didn't blame the car owner for roughing up Andrew – you'd probably react the same way). You'd been working desperately this year to improve the public image of the school – and now this! The stress has affected you physically – you've been sick, you had to take leave the day following the incident, and you have been finding it difficult to concentrate. You're impressed by how supportive the parents have been of the school's actions.

PETER MANNING (car owner)

You were shocked by the incident and extremely angry – so angry that you 'lost it' when you caught one of the boys. You were worried about your family in the car (wife, parents and three-year-old daughter) who could all have been injured or killed. You were extremely put out by the expense of repairs (windscreen) and were pleased that the families of the boys have offered to pay for the replacement so that you don't lose your no-claim insurance discount. Your daughter is now wetting the bed at night and is frightened of getting into the car. Your parents are elderly and your father has a heart condition. You're sorry in retrospect if you frightened Andrew too much, but felt at the time that he needed to be taught a lesson. You feel sorry for the school having to deal with the incident and the way the school's reputation has suffered.

CONSTABLE BROWN (police officer)

You were at the station and took the initial statements when Mr Manning (the car owner) drove Andrew to the police station straight after the incident. You saw first hand how terrified and shaken the occupants of the car were. You attended a similar accident some years ago in which the driver's wife was killed, and the driver himself suffered serious and permanent injuries as they collided with another car. This incident has reminded you of the horrors of that case, and you want to make sure that the boys take this matter seriously and that they learn their lesson for once and for all. Provided that you see the right attitudes from the boys and their families, and provided that the victim is happy to resolve the matter informally, you are willing to go along with their agreement. While it is important that this kind of thing does not happen again in the future, you would not wish to see the boys' future being jeopardised because of their stupid behaviour on this particular occasion. You want to see them learn from it.

JANE HIGGINS (school counsellor)

You hadn't too much involvement with the boys to date, but had known that the ninth grade coordinator had worked a lot with Andrew. Your main concern is that the boys settle down into school and at home, and if there was support required to achieve that, you want the boys to feel free to come to you and talk things over at any time.

BRIAN COURTNEY (ninth grade year coordinator)

You had been alerted by teachers that the boys were missing from class – on returning to the school, the two boys told you that Andrew had been beaten up and taken away by an angry motorist. You were frantic about Andrew.

One of your roles at the school is to monitor behaviour/attendance etc, and you are particularly disappointed in the boys, especially Andrew, who you've invested a lot of time with. It has frustrated you and made you unhappy and short tempered, even at home.

MR JOHNSON (Mark's father)

You are shocked that one of your kids could do such a thing. You have felt shame, anger and disbelief. You feel you can no longer trust Mark. You are devastated at the thought of what the consequences could have been. You can totally understand Mr Manning's (the car owner) anger. You can't believe the thoughtlessness of the act. You were quick to contact the car owner and offer to pay for the new windscreen.

MARK JOHNSON (Ninth grade student)

You didn't want to go to class, so you and the others decided to wag. You went to the overpass, threw rocks, hit a car, got very scared and hid in the bushes. You were especially frightened by what happened to Andrew. You've been grounded at home as well as suspended from school. You reckon the people in the car were probably pretty disgusted. Your parents are shocked and the school's reputation has been affected.

MRS JOHNSON (Mark's mother)

You were absolutely stunned by the news of the incident and just couldn't believe it. You are disappointed and deeply ashamed. You are also angry at the risk that Mark took and the danger he caused. Mark is now grounded and has some privileges removed. You are very worried about him, but no longer sure that you can trust him.

DONALD JEFFRIES (Ninth grade student)

You wagged with your friends, walked to the overpass and started throwing stones. You were very frightened and really worried to see Andrew being pushed into the car. Back at school, you laid low till you saw the police car arrive with Andrew, then you decided to "give yourself up". You knew that throwing stones at cars was a dangerous thing to do. Your parents are disappointed, you've been grounded and made to do more chores around the house. You understand how easily people could have been injured, and know that you may have given your school a bad name.

SARA JEFFRIES (Donald's sister)

You initially heard about the incident on the bus going home, but heard lots of different stories, so didn't know what to believe. Don wasn't on the bus and you didn't know what to make of that. You felt physically sick when you heard the whole story. You were worried about what could have happened. Things have been so bad at home that you can't bear to be there. You make veiled hints at the possibility of Dad beating up Don (there have been other occasions) and at this point you cry and tell Don you love him and are really worried for him.

ANDREW SMITH (Ninth grade student)

You wagged with your friends, walked to the overpass and started throwing stones. One of you managed to hit a car. You got scared, ran and hid in the bushes, but the owner caught you and handled you roughly. He did not actually punch you, but he was really angry. The car owner took you to the police station. The police brought you back to school. You're in trouble now, suspended from school and grounded at home. You were very frightened by the incident, especially by the man's anger, and by being taken to the police station.

You know how your mum has been affected – disappointed and angry. The people in the car were angry and the Principal is annoyed.

MRS SMITH (Andrew's mother)

Your initial reactions were shock and disappointment, then you were very angry. You were also extremely worried about Andrew having being manhandled by the car owner and taken away by him to the police station (even thought you could understand how angry the car owner must have been). Since then, everyone at home has been upset and things have been pretty tense.

Sexual assault and harassment:
A role play

Developed by Charles Barton at Charles Sturt University

FACILITATOR'S MASTER GUIDE

The incident – case description

While on an overseas detachment, Julie was accommodated with her fellow officers. She was the only female in the Unit. One evening in the Officer's Mess one of the male officers, Michael, who is present, grabbed her breast. In a reflexive action she threw her drink into his chest. The officer braced himself and pulled his fist back to hit her, but he did not strike her.

The incident was witnessed by a Commanding Officer of an RAAF flying unit (LTCOL equivalent) who walked away without commenting, intervening, or speaking to the officer who assaulted her. (This officer chose not to attend.)

The matter has been investigated and confirmed by Jeff, who is present. This conference is an attempt to deal, on an informal basis, with the complaint and the disruption caused by the incident.

Instruction to participants

This is an educational role play. Please keep fairly close to your assigned role, and try playing it realistically, especially when it comes to filling in the gaps in the script. Do not read out your role all in one go. The facilitator will prompt you for the relevant information at appropriate times. If you feel that your particular role, or the role play as a whole, is not realistic, you should raise your concerns in discussion afterwards. Disruption of the role-play diminishes its educational impact.

De-roling and debriefing

Immediately after the role play, and while participants are still seated, go around the circle and ask each person:

- their real name
- one thing which is different about them from the role they played
- any insights they might have gained from playing that role

Sexual assault seating plan

Director of Personnel

Michael's close friend
and colleague

Michael's wife

Offender

Michael's son

Michael's
Commanding Officer

David

Amanda

Michael

Andrew

Mark

Jim

Facilitator

Jeff

Mary

Bill

Susan

Julie

Investigating officer

Julie's friend

Julie's fellow officer
and witness

Harassment Officer

Complainant/victim

ROLE DESCRIPTIONS FOR PARTICIPANTS

MARY (Julie's friend from outside Defence)

You understand Julie's anger, having experienced harassment yourself. You are here to support her and to tell the meeting about the consequences that the incident has had in her life and yours (for example, bringing back distressing memories).

JULIE (victim of the assault)

You were shaken by the incident, particularly as nobody seemed to take it seriously at the time. Your complaint seems to create unease in the Unit and Michael especially has been putting pressure on you to drop the case. However, while you find the atmosphere in the Unit unpleasant and very stressful, you do not want to condone the behaviour.

In terms of an outcome, you want a sincere acknowledgement from Michael and other senior officers of the distress caused to you, and an apology from Michael for his behaviour.

SUSAN (Harassment Officer)

You have supported Julie's complaint and are supportive of her whichever way she wishes this incident resolved. You have seen how badly she has been affected and her case is not uncommon. You wish something was done to prevent these kinds of incidents from happening.

BILL (fellow officer who witnessed the event)

You have been very unsettled about this incident and while you do not approve of this kind of behaviour, the incident and the complaint have created a lot of tension in the Unit, dividing people who were previously good colleagues. (For example, while some people support Julie, many others think that she should drop the case – they feel that it reflects badly on the Unit.)

JEFF (investigating officer)

You have heard both sides of the story and support both parties in resolving the matter informally. You have seen the tremendous harm suffered by everybody as a result of this incident.

JIM (Director of Personnel)

You were disturbed by the incident and agreed to attend in order to gain a better view of what is happening in the organisation. This incident indicates to you that proper training in this area is required.

To help repair the damage, you volunteer a *personal* apology to the victim for what happened and assure her that you will take steps to prevent things like this happening in the future.

DAVID (Michael's close friend and colleague)

You agree that Michael behaved foolishly and insensitively. You support him in putting things back on track. The victim's (Julie) account helped you realise just how serious these kinds of things are. You commit to help changing the culture informally by discouraging sexist jokes and attitudes in the unit.

AMANDA (Michael's wife)

You are very upset and angry about what happened and are in the process of trying to work things out with Michael who assures you that this was out of character and that it will never happen again. Trust is the main issue for you and it will take time for Michael to regain it.

You also wonder if Julie might not have been flirting at work which might have precipitated the incident.

MICHAEL (offender)

You admit that you had too much to drink on the night. At first you play down the significance of the incident, and you certainly intended no harm. (It was more like a prank? Or an accident? Please improvise realistically.)

The incident and the rumours caused problems for you at home and you are trying to work things out. You are not sure how Andrew, your 22-year-old son, is feeling about the whole thing, but he is present, as is your wife.

Also, you tried to convince Julie to drop the case against you, which may have put pressure on her at work, adding to her distress.

This may have been a mistake but the whole thing was spiralling out of control.

ANDREW (Michael's 22-year-old son)

You are training to be a pilot and are deeply embarrassed by the incident. The rumours are making things very awkward at work. While fundamentally you respect your father, you are disturbed by his behaviour. Also, you care a lot about how this is affecting your mother, and their marriage.

MARK (Michael's Commanding Officer)

Michael is a competent officer and you have always had full trust in him. You consider this incident to be most regrettable, but you are prepared to accept Michael's assurances that it will never happen again. The incident created division among your staff and the air is thick with tension. You have been slow to appreciate it at first, but acknowledge that Julie has been well within her rights in not having let matters rest. However, you also want this destructive situation sorted out.

For training purposes you can obtain the fully developed and prepared versions of these and other role plays, complete with tailored facilitation prompts based on the Empowerment Model of group conference facilitation. They are available online from the publisher at <www.federationpress.com.au>

Bibliography

Abel, CF and Marsh, FH, 1984, *Punishment and Restitution: A Restitutionary Approach to Crime and the Criminal*, Westport: Greenwood Press.

Alder, C and Wundersitz, J (eds), 1994, *Family Conferencing and Juvenile Justice: The Way Forward, or Misplaced Optimism?* Canberra: Australian Institute of Criminology.

Bandura, A, 1990, 'Mechanisms of Moral Disengagement', in *Origins of Terrorism*, W Reich (ed), Cambridge: Woodrow Wilson International Center for Scholars and Cambridge University Press.

Barton, C, 1996, *Revenge and Victim Justice*, PhD Thesis, Australian National University, Canberra (later published as Barton 1999a).

Barton, C, 1999a, *Getting Even: Revenge as a Form of Justice*, Chicago and La Salle: Open Court Publishing.

Barton, C, 1999b, 'Empowerment and Retribution in Criminal Justice', *Res Publica* 8: 16-23. (Also published in Strang, H and Braithwaite, J, 2000, *Restorative Justice: From Philosophy to Practice*, Aldershot: Dartmouth; *Journal of Professional Ethics*, 7, 3&4: 111-35.

Barton, C, 2000, 'Restorative Justice Empowerment', *The Australian Journal of Professional and Applied Ethics* 2, 2: 16-31. (Also published in Warwick Tie (ed) *Just Peace: Peace Making and Peace Building for the New Millennium*, Conference Proceedings, 24-28 April 2000, Massey University, Albany, NZ: Massey University Centre for Justice and Peace Development (pp 50-62)).

Barton, C, 2000a, '*Getting Even* Again: A Reply to Davis', *International Journal of Applied Philosophy* 14, 1: 129-42.

Barton, C, 2000b, 'Theories of Restorative Justice', *The Australian Journal of Professional and Applied Ethics* 2, 1: 41-53. Also published in Warwick Tie (ed) *Just Peace: Peace Making and Peace Building for the New Millennium*, Conference Proceedings, 24-28 April 2000, Massey University, Albany, NZ: Massey University Centre for Justice and Peace Development (pp 63-73).

Barton, C, 2001, 'Victim-Offender and Community Empowerment: A New Paradigm in Criminal Justice', *International Journal of Applied Philosophy* 15, 1: 25-46.

Barton, C, 2002, 'Revenge Rights in Criminal Justice', *The Australian Journal of Professional and Applied Ethics* 4, 1: 53-59.

Barton, C and van den Broek, K, 1999, 'Restorative Justice Conferencing and the Ethic of Care', *Ethics and Justice* 2: 55-65.

Bazemore, G and Schiff, M (eds), 2001, *Restorative Community Justice: Repairing Harm and Transforming Communities,* Cincinnati: Anderson Publishing Co.

Bird, S, 1998, *Conference Convenor Training Package,* Sydney: Department of Juvenile Justice.

Boyack, J, 1999, 'How Sayest the Court of Appeal?' in Consedine and Bowen (eds), *Restorative Justice: Contemporary Themes and Practice,* Lyttleton, NZ: Ploughshares Publications.

Braithwaite, J, 1989, *Crime, Shame and Reintegration,* Cambridge: Cambridge University Press.

Braithwaite, J, 1996, *Restorative Justice and a Better Future,* Dorothy J, Killam Memorial Lecture, Dalhousie University, 17 October.

Braithwaite, J and Mugford, S, 1994, 'Conditions of Successful Reintegration Ceremonies', *British Journal of Criminology* 34: 139-171.

Braithwaite, J and Pettit, P, 1990, *Not Just Deserts,* Oxford: Clarendon.

Braithwaite, J, 2002, *Restorative Justice and Responsive Regulation,* New York: Oxford University Press.

Braithwaite, J, 2003, 'Principles of Restorative Justice', in von Hirsch et al (eds) *Restorative Justice and Criminal Justice,* Oxford and Portland, Oregon: Hart Publishing

Braithwaite, J and Roche, D, 2001, 'Responsibility and Restorative Justice', in Bazemore and Schiff (eds) *Restorative Community Justice: Repairing Harm and Transforming Communities,* Cincinnati: Anderson Publishing Co.

Brown, BJ and McElrea, FWM, (eds) 1993, *The Youth Court in New Zealand: A New Model of Justice,* Publication No 34, Auckland: Legal Research Foundation.

Consedine, J (ed), 1995, *Restorative Justice: Healing the Effects of Crime,* Lyttleton, NZ: Ploughshares Publications.

Consedine, J and Bowen, H (eds), 1999, *Restorative Justice: Contemporary Themes and Practice,* Lyttleton, NZ: Ploughshares Publications.

Daly, K, 1989, 'Criminal Justice Ideologies and Practices in Different Voices: Some Feminist Questions about Justice', *International Journal of the Sociology of Law* 17: 1-18.

Davis, M, 2000, 'Revenge, Victim Rights, and Criminal Justice', *International Journal of Applied Philosophy* 14, 1: 119-128.

Davis, M, 2001, 'Victim Rights, Revenge, and Retribution', *The Australian Journal of Professional and Applied Ethics* 3, 2: 45-68.

Dignan, J and Cavadino, M, 1996, 'Toward a Framework for Conceptualising and Evaluating Models of Criminal Justice from a Victim's Perspective', *International Review of Victimology* 4: 153-182.

Galaway, B and Hudson, J (eds), 1996, *Restorative Justice: International Perspectives,* New York: Criminal Justice Press.

Giuliano, B (ed), 1998, *Survival and Beyond: An Anthology of Stories by Victims of Crime and a Victims Resource Guide,* Canberra: The National Association for Loss and Grief, ACT Inc.

Harding, J, 1982, *Victims and Offenders,* London: Bedford Square Press.

Hudson, J, Morris, A, Maxwell, G, Galaway, B, (eds) 1996, *Family Group Conferences: Perspectives on Policy and Practice,* Sydney: The Federation Press.

Jones, K, 1996, *Restorative Justice: The Theoretical Dream of Idealism,* LLB (Hons) Research Paper; Criminal Law and Procedure (LAWS 511) Law Faculty, Victoria University of Wellington, New Zealand.

Kelly, DP, 1990, 'Victim Participation in the Criminal Justice System', in AJ Lurigio, WA Skogan and RC Davis (eds), *Victims of Crime: Problems, Policies and Programs,* California: Sage.

Long, K, 1995, 'Community Input at Sentencing: Victim's Right or Victim's Revenge', *Boston University Law Review* 75: 187-229.

Maxwell, G and Morris, A, 1993, *Family, Victims and Culture: Youth Justice in New Zealand,* Wellington: Social Policy Agency and Institute of Criminology, Victoria University of Wellington.

Maxwell, G and Morris, A, 1996, 'Research on Family Group Conferences with Young Offenders in New Zealand', in Hudson et al, *Family Group Conferences: Perspectives on Policy and Practice,* Sydney: The Federation Press.

Maxwell, G, 1998, 'Researching Reoffending: Recent Research on Family Group Conferences', Conference Proceedings, *Youth Justice in Focus,* Wellington: Victoria University of Wellington, October.

McCarthy, T, 1994, 'Victim Impact Statements: A Problematic Remedy', *Australian Feminist Law Journal* 3: 175-195.

McDonald, J, Moore, D, O'Connell, T and Thorsborne, M, 1995, 'Coordinating Family Group Conferences', in B Wachtel and T Wachtel, *Real Justice™ Training Manual,* Pipersville: The Piper's Press.

McElrea, FWM, 1993, 'A New Model of Justice', in Brown and McElrea (eds), *The Youth Court in New Zealand: A New Model of Justice,* Publication No 34, Auckland: Legal Research Foundation.

McElrea, FWM, 1996, *Rape: Ten Years Progress?* Address to the Interdisciplinary Conference, Wellington, 29 March.

McElrea, FWM, 1999, Taking Responsibility in Being Accountable, In Consedine and Bowen (eds), *Restorative Justice: Contemporary Themes and Practice,* Lyttleton, NZ: Ploughshares Publications.

Moore, D, 1993, 'Shame, Forgiveness and Juvenile Justice', *Criminal Justice Ethics* 12: 3 -25.

Moore, D, 1995, *A New Approach to Juvenile Justice: An Evaluation of Family Conferences in Wagga Wagga – A Report to the Criminology Research Council,* Wagga Wagga: Charles Sturt University.

Morris, A and Maxwell, G, 1997, 'Family Group Conferences and Convictions', *Occasional Papers in Criminology,* New Series: No 5, Wellington: Institute of Criminology, Victoria University of Wellington.

Morris, A and Young, W, 1999, 'Reforming Criminal Justice: The Potential of Restorative Justice', Presented to the Conference: *Restorative Justice and Civil Society,* Canberra, Australian National University, February.

Munn, M, 1993, 'Restorative Justice: An Alternative to Vengeance', *American Journal of Criminal Law* 20: 99.

O'Connell, T, 1996, *Police and Personal Accountability: Shame, the Missing Dimension,* Sydney: Human Resources Command, NSW Police Service.

O'Connell, T, 1997, 'Dawn or Dusk in Sentencing: Rediscovering the Human Face of Justice', Presentation to CIAJ National Conference, Quebec.

O'Connell, T and The Restorative Justice Group, 1998, *Community Accountability Conferencing: Coordinator Training Manual,* Sydney: Human Resources Command, NSW Police Service.

Palk, G, Hayes, H and Prenzler, T, 1998, 'Restorative Justice and Community Conferencing: Summary of Findings from a Pilot Study', *Current Issues in Criminal Justice* 10: 138-155.

R v Clotworthy (1998) 15 CRNZ 651 (Appeal Court of New Zealand 114/98, Wellington, New Zealand).

Retzinger, SM and Scheff, TJ, 1996, 'Strategy for Community Conferences: Emotions and Social Bonds', in B Galaway and J Hudson (eds), *Restorative Justice: International Perspectives,* Monsey, NY: Criminal Justice Press.

RISE Working Papers 1997, Papers #1–#4, *A Series of Reports on Research in Progress on the Reintergrative Shaming Experiment (RISE) for Restorative Community Policing,* Canberra: Law Program, Research School of Social Sciences, Australian National University.

Shermann, L, Strang, H and Barnes, J, 1997, *Reintegrative Shaming Experiment Results,* Canberra: Australian National University.

Shermann, L, Strang, H, Barnes, J, Braithwaite, J, Inkpen, N and Teh, M, 1998, *Experiments in Restorative Policing: A Progress Report,* Canberra: Law Program, Research School of Social Sciences, Australian National University.

Thornton, C, 1993, *Family Group Conferences: A Literature Review,* New Zealand: Practitioners' Publishing.

Tuhiwai Smith, L and Cram, F, 1998, *An Evaluation of the Community Panel Diversion Pilot Programme,* Auckland: Auckland Uniservices Limited University of Auckland.

Umbreit, MS, 1989, 'Crime Victims Seeking Fairness, Not Revenge: Towards Restorative Justice', *Federal Probation* 53: 52–57.

Van Ness, DW, 1990, 'Restoring the Balance: Tipping the Scales of Justice', *Corrections Today* 52: 62–66.

Van Ness, DW, 1996, 'Restorative Justice and International Human Rights', in Galaway, B and Hudson, J (eds), 1996, *Restorative Justice: International Perspectives,* New York: Criminal Justice Press.

Van Ness, DW, 1997, *Restoring Justice,* Cincinnati: Anderson.

von Hirsch, A, Roberts J, Bottoms, A, Roach, K and Schiff, M (eds), 2003, *Restorative Justice and Criminal Justice,* Oxford and Portland, Oregon: Hart Publishing.

von Willigenburg, T, 1996, 'Criminals and Moral Development: Towards a cognitive theory of moral change', in H Tam (ed), *Punishment, Excuses and Moral Development,* Brookfield: Ashgate Publishing Company.

Walgrave, L, 1995, 'Restorative Justice for Juveniles: Just a Technique or a Fully Fledged Alternative?' *The Howard Journal* 34: 228-49.

Wright, M, 1991, *Justice for Victims and Offenders: A Restorative Response to Crime,* Philadelphia: Open University Press.

Wright, M, 1996, *Justice for Victims and Offenders: A Restorative Response to Crime,* 2nd edn, Winchester: Waterside Press, (first published 1991).

Wundersitz, J and Hetzel, S, 1996, 'Family Conferences for Young Offenders: The South Australian Experience', in Hudson et al, *Family Group Conferences: Perspectives on Policy and Practice,* Sydney: The Federation Press.

Zehr, H, 1990, *Changing Lenses,* Scottdale: Harold Press.

Index